Texas Wildflowers

University of Texas Press
Austin

Texas Wildflowers

A FIELD GUIDE

by Campbell and Lynn Loughmiller

Lynn Sherrod, Technical Editor

Foreword by Lady Bird Johnson

Tenth paperback printing, 2002

Requests for permission to reproduce material
from this work should be sent to:
Permissions
University of Texas Press
Post Office Box 7819
Austin, Texas 78713-7819

LIBRARY OF CONGRESS
CATALOGING IN PUBLICATION DATA

Loughmiller, Campbell
    Texas wildflowers

    Bibliography: p.
    Includes index.
    1. Wild flowers—Texas   Identification
I. Loughmiller, Lynn.   II. Sherrod, Lynn.   III. Title.
QK188.L68   1984   582.13′09764   83-10624
ISBN 0-292-78059-1
ISBN 0-292-78060-5 (pbk.)

Contents

Foreword

I WELCOME this new field guide for Texas wildflower enthusiasts.

Just reading the text and seeing the beautiful color photographs—all 381 of them—makes me want to reach for my sunhat, put on my walking shoes, take this knowledge-filled book and fare forth to seek and discover!

That is exactly what the authors—Campbell and Lynn Loughmiller—have been doing for forty years. I had the fun of hearing about their wildflower adventures first-hand.

"We load our trailer with typewriter, cameras, sunburn lotion, and insect repellent, and we just set out. We don't know where we are heading and we don't care where we spend the night," the Loughmillers explained.

How wonderful to own your own time, and let instinct lead you to the flowerscapes that abide in Texas, from the phlox of South Texas to the wonderful world of cactus in West Texas!

The authors have traveled and photographed hundreds of beautiful field scenes and then knelt down for close-ups of the "inhabitants." Selecting the ones for this book from a vast array of color slides was a "terrible task, like choosing among your grandchildren," they told me.

Their trails brought them to the University of Texas Press, and into publication with this stunning and useful field guide which has been ably reviewed for technical accuracy by Dr. Lynn Sherrod, botanist at the University of Texas at Tyler.

We share a sense of poetry among the wildflowers. To borrow from Wordsworth, I gasp and "my heart with rapture fills" when I come upon a pasture filled with bluebonnets set among the feathery pale green of mesquite trees in spring, and beyond, the gnarled and twisted live oaks—the scene punctuated by exclamation points of brilliant coral Indian paintbrush and white Mexican poppies!

One of the favorite pastimes of my childhood was to walk in the woods of East Texas, exploring, particularly in the springtime. I knew where the first wild violets bloomed, and looked for the dogwood—those white blossoms, like stars spangling the bare woods. And I hunted for the delicate wild roses that grew along the fences in the rural farm country where I grew up. Ever since, I have had a love affair with nature I have never ceased to savor. It has enriched my life and provided me with beautiful, serene memories. For me, wildflowers have been part of the joy of living.

We all have our favorite highway strips and fields to explore in springtime, but with this book, we discover wildflower hunting—*somewhere* in Texas—is an activity for extended seasons. For instance, in July, I came upon graceful wands of gleaming red Standing Cypress—now mostly along steep embankments and fence rows where the June mowing had not obliterated them before their blooming season. Will they disappear forever from the Texas scene?

Last September, I walked on a meadow near the LBJ Ranch and saw the embroidery of snow-on-the-mountain among the waving grasses, and in the distance the blue mist of the river valley and the purple spikes of gay feathers brightening the roadsides. What poetry! There are so many delicious surprises that come when we are rich with rain. I yearn to see, identify, and cultivate more of the flowers for late summer and fall.

It is a truism that the more you learn, the more you want to learn. This book leads one on and on. I gradually find myself reaching for the botanical name and translating the ones I do not know. My mail tells me there are thousands of people who share my enthusiasm for wildflowers and hunger to know more. Take this book in hand and experience the delight of coming upon a scarlet bloom along a stream bank and tracking it through the book to its identity: the cardinal flower!

My world of wildflowers is expanding each day with the National Wildflower Research Center, which we founded in December 1982 on a farm-to-market road near Austin. There, I hope we will learn about germination, growth habits, where and how to plant the treasure trove of wildflowers both for their aesthetic and conservation potential. As a practical person, I want to know more of the simple "how-to's"—and, yes, the "how-not-to's." I hope very much we can make such information available to the expanding constituency of those who care.

I am so grateful for the unflagging pursuit of the Lough-millers, and to the University of Texas Press for its timely publication and for its generosity in sharing the sales of this book with the Wildflower Center.

Lady Bird Johnson
Honorary Co-Chairman
National Wildflower Research Center

Introduction   This book has grown out of our long-standing interest in wild-flowers and our increasing appreciation of the extraordinary diversity we have found as we photographed them in all parts of the state. The varied topography, soil types, rainfall, and temperature combine to give Texas more than 5,000 species. They are found from elevations of 8,000 feet in the Guadalupe Mountains of West Texas to the subtropical Rio Grande Valley near sea level, and from the Chihuahuan Desert to Southeast Texas where the annual rainfall is 56 inches.

We were tempted to include as many as possible of the larger, showier, more colorful species, as well as those harbingers of spring, the violets, bluets, and others, which have, since our childhood, promised the end of winter and the beginning of longer, brighter, warmer days. While the reader will find here many of these favorites, we have also tried to include in our selection representative specimens from all parts of the state.

We were impressed by the fact that the inconspicuous flowers often grow where nothing else is to be found. It is an arresting sight when, on the rocky slopes of the sun-baked Chihuahuan desert, for example, one comes across the delicately beautiful four-nerved daisy or the prickleleaf gilia. Somehow their appeal is magnified by the stark setting.

People the world over draw satisfaction from studying, classifying, collecting, sketching, photographing, or simply observing wildflowers. When circumstances deprive us of this pleasure we begin to understand how much a part of our lives flowers are—as integral and rewarding as bird songs, blue skies, rainshowers, the smell of rich earth, or the crispness of a change of seasons.

We have attempted to organize this book for a broad audience, for what we might describe as the interested layperson. As with all scientific disciplines, botany has of necessity developed its own professional language. For the professional that scheme is necessary and valuable, but too many laypersons get lost in terminology when they must wade through it in order to make the simplest identification. A lapful of dictionaries, textbooks, and glossaries is neither essential nor especially conducive to the enjoyment of flowers. We have included a short glossary of terms which are regularly used to make descriptions of flowers more meaningful and precise. These terms should not distract one from the purpose of the book which is to promote the recognition and enjoyment of wildflowers.

It is our hope that the organization will prove satisfactory both for readers seeking no more than a quick confirmation of

a plant's identity and for those embarking upon a more sophis-
ticated study.

Identification of flowers down through family and genus is
rarely very difficult, but determining the species can be tedious, and often frustrating. This is true for the scientist as
well as the knowledgeable amateur. In the preparation of this
book we have sometimes found disagreement between eminent
scientists as to the classification of flowers. It has extended not
only to the species, but sometimes to the genus, and occasionally even to the family. For example, there are many species of
Verbena in Texas. Some of them differ so slightly that no amateur could detect any difference whatever, nor could the scientist, either, without a microscope. Based on these minute
variations, a flower is assigned to one species or another. Over
a period of time, however, botanists finally come to a common
agreement about most plants. In the process, old classifications
sometimes disappear and are replaced by new ones.

This should not discourage the amateur, however, who may
find the genus to be sufficiently definitive. Should one's interest carry one further, a 10× hand lens will be helpful in all
cases, essential in some.

Though books such as this one typically devote much space
to matters of plant classification, it is not necessary to know
the name of a flower in order to appreciate it. People drive
hundreds of miles in favorable years to see the desert floor in
bloom, or to enjoy a high mountain meadow ablaze with the
brief, intense colors of summer, without knowing the name
of a single flower they see—and they are amply rewarded. A
personal experience one spring made this point convincingly
as we stopped to see a man and his wife in a lonely location
surrounded by forty miles of desert. The husband was not
there, and his wife told us, "Bill rode up the canyon this morning to see if the wildflowers are blooming." He returned shortly
with a small bouquet he had gathered. These people knew the
flowers—knew them more completely and appreciated them
more fully than most persons we have known; where they
grew, when they bloomed, their size, shape, color, markings,
and other details. We realized again that it is better to know
the nature of a flower than its name.

Still, most people want to know the names of flowers, as this
facilitates communication and seems to bring them closer to
us. If they do not know the name they will give it one; hence,
the many common names. Since common names vary from
one place to another, they are not useful to denote particular
plants. We have included common names but have also used

the Latin names, which are definitive and do not vary from place to place.

The distribution of flowers over the state is constantly changing because their seeds are dispersed by wind, water, birds, animals, automobiles, and other agents. We can describe the general areas where different species grow, but a flower is often found well beyond its generally accepted range. Simply put, a flower grows where you find it. The Texas Highway Department has done a fine job of seeding the wide rights-of-ways along our highways with native flowers, and does not mow the vegetation until after the flowers have gone to seed. This has resulted in a remarkable floral display in many areas of the state. Even in areas never touched by human efforts at reseeding, numbers of species can be found along every road. They may not be obvious to people who are hurrying from Here to There; but those who take a break and step out of their automobiles will be surprised, if not refreshed, at the display almost at their feet. We have often stopped in the most un-likely places—what some would call "waste places"—and have rarely gone unrewarded.

Blooming periods also vary, and many times a species that blooms in the spring will bloom again in the fall if the mois-ture and temperature are favorable. This is especially true in Southwest Texas, where the blooming period is often related as much to moisture as it is to the season of the year. Sometimes a species will disappear from the landscape and not be seen for several years, but under favorable conditions it will reappear in impressive numbers.

Pollination of flowers is an important process, both to the flower and to the insect that accomplishes it. Insects are at-tracted to flowers by their color, fragrance, or nectar. It is inter-esting that colorful, conspicuous flowers are seldom fragrant, as fragrance is not necessary for them to attract insects. The honeybee is perhaps the best-known insect in the pollinating process, assisting the plant and making honey at the same time. Farmers are glad to pay beekeepers to put bees in their crops as it increases the yield substantially. To us, however, butterflies are more interesting, as they are sometimes as beau-tiful as the flowers. In photographing the flowers of some spe-cies, we often ended up spending more time photographing the butterflies that were attracted to them.

One of the most specific relationships in the pollinating pro-cess is that of the *Yucca* and the *Pronuba* moth, which have become so interdependent that neither can survive without the other. The moth does not visit the flowers of any other species but makes sure it pollinates this one well. It gathers a ball of pollen from one flower and deposits it on the pistil of another, even rubbing it in with its head after laying its eggs half an inch below. When the larvae develop they feed on the seed. Of the thirty or so species of *Yucca*, of which Texas has several, all except one depend on a species of the *Pronuba* moth for pollination, a different species for each species. The moth does not eat the pollen or the nectar, but the larvae live in the plant's ovary, thus perpetuating their own species and that of the *Yucca*. No moth, no *Yucca*, and vice versa.

Many flowers close at night, some by day. We had an interesting experience with one of them—*Hibiscus lasiocarpus*, or false cotton—late one afternoon when we stopped to photograph it. Several of the blossoms had already closed so tightly that it seemed as if they had never opened. Carefully we pulled the petals apart on one of them to see how they overlapped each other, and when we lifted the last petal we found a bumblebee right in the center. We opened seven others and found bumblebees in five of them. We did not know whether they had chosen the flowers as a good place to spend the night or whether they had inadvertently stayed past closing time and were trapped.

All of our photographs were taken in the field where the flowers grew in their natural environment. We like to show their natural habitat, to put them "in their place." Usually we take two pictures—one of the whole plant, and a close-up of the flower. This has presented some difficult choices in selecting pictures for this book, as we could not include both.

Photography is always rewarding but can sometimes be tedious. When, for instance, one is photographing a West Texas flower in March, and a strong wind whips the long-stemmed flower 180 degrees in a fitful dance for five minutes without let-up, and you wait for that one fleeting instant when it comes to a dead stop, with the merciless sun burning your face as you wait—well, it takes all of one's patience and half one's religion to maintain equanimity. At that point, there is a good argument for removing the flower to a protected area and composing the picture in leisurely comfort.

In East Texas it is much the same. You set up for a picture only to find you are knee-deep in grassburs, that you have aroused a mound of fire ants or brushed against a nettle, or that you have become host to chiggers, ticks, or mosquitoes. But then, what satisfaction would there be in walking up to a flower on a calm, clear day, setting up the tripod and "pulling the trigger"?

Many wildflowers are suitable for gardens, and we have mentioned some of these in the text. Persons interested in using them in home landscaping will find many seed companies that specialize in wildflower seeds. The National Wildflower Research Center, 2600 FM 973 North, Austin, Texas 78725, serves as a clearing house for information on seed collection, commercial sources, and wildflower propagation.

The flowers and their descriptions are arranged alphabetically by families according to their scientific names. Readers may get to know some of the general characteristics of each group, especially the larger ones, that will help in identifying individual flowers. We have not included a key to identification, as such a key presupposes considerable training in botany and is difficult for the layperson to use. All common and scientific plant names used in the book are included in the index. The book also contains an illustrated glossary of flower parts and botanical terms.

We have indicated in the text the area where each flower was photographed. The range is general and is intended to show the approximate boundaries within which a species grows.

Most of the flowers shown are of herbaceous plants, but we have also included those of many shrubs and woody vines and a few trees.

CAMPBELL LOUGHMILLER

Acknowledgments

We express our appreciation to Lynn
Sherrod, Barton H. Warnock, and Marshall
Johnston for their help in identifying
many of the flowers we photographed; and
to Del Weniger and Harry Barwick for
their help in identifying some of the cacti.
We should also like to acknowledge the
help Lance Rosier (deceased) gave us in
locating and identifying many flowers
of the Big Thicket.

Texas Wildflowers

ACANTHACEAE
Acanthus or Wild Petunia Family

The Acanthus Family includes trees, shrubs, and herbs. Stems are square; leaves are generally without teeth or lobes, and are opposite. The blue, lavender, or purple flowers are 2-lipped and almost radially symmetrical. There are 2–4 stamens; when 4, they are in unequal pairs. *Ruellia*, or wild petunia, is our most common genus.

Ruellia nudiflora
Wild Petunia

The wild petunia has flowers much like those of the cultivated petunia (genus *Petunia*, family Solanaceae). The plants are erect, 1–2 feet tall, with few branches. The leaves are opposite, 2–5 inches long, narrowed at the base, on short stems. At the top of the plant are several trumpet-shaped, purplish blossoms that are nearly 2 inches across at the opening. They open shortly after sunrise, lasting only one day. This one was photographed near Huntsville in June. *Common in open woods or prairies in East, Central, and South Texas. April–June. Perennial.*

Dyschoriste linearis
Narrowleaf Dyschoriste (Snake Herb)

Several erect stems, 6–12 inches tall, grow from the root of this plant; the branches and stems are covered with stiff, coarse hairs. The leaves are opposite, ¾–2¾ inches long, attached directly to the 4-sided stem. The 2-lipped flowers are ½–1 inch long and up to 1 inch across, lavender to purple, with purple stripes in the throat. They grow in the leaf axils on very short stems and are somewhat tucked in between the leaves, scattered here and there on the main stem. This one was photographed in the Davis Mountains in July. *Central and West Texas. June–October.*

There are many other species of *Ruellia* in Texas. One of them, *R. caroliniensis*, grows to 18 inches tall, with opposite leaves, 2–3½ inches long; margins are wavy or vaguely toothed. Flowers are purplish-blue, single or in small clusters in the upper leaf axils. *East Texas (west to Dallas). April–September. Perennial.*

ALISMATACEAE
Water-Plantain or Arrowhead Family

Members of the Water-Plantain Family
grow in water, in swamps, on muddy
banks, or occasionally in wet sand. Each
plant has long-petioled leaves in a clump
with a flowering stem rising among them.
The flowers have 3 green sepals, 3 white or
pink-tinged petals, 6 or more stamens, and
several pistils. Stamens and pistils may be
in separate flowers.

Sagittaria falcata
Arrowhead (Duck Potato)

The genus *Sagittaria* gets its name from
the arrow-shaped leaves of some species,
though the leaves of *S. falcata* are long
and narrow. The flowers are quite distinctive, with 3 green sepals and 3 white petals, ¼–½ inch long. The pistils often are
flattened and form a tight, round green
center. The tubers and young shoots
which grow in the mud are said to have
been a staple food of the Indians. Early set-
tlers called them duck potatoes because
they are a favorite food of ducks.

   One or more species of *Sagittaria* can be
found in any section of Texas that has
ponds, swamps, muddy shallows, lazy
streams, or even roadside ditches. The 3-
petaled white flowers and the swampy locations are good clues to their identity. It
is very difficult to distinguish one species
from another. *Statewide. July–October.
Perennial.*

—————————————————————

Another plant in the same family, with
blossoms resembling those of the arrowhead, grows under similar conditions: the
burhead, *Echinodorus cordifolius*. It grows
to 4 feet high and is often arched or lying
on the ground. *April–June. Perennial.*

AMARANTHACEAE
Pigweed Family

The Amaranthaceae are a family of annual or perennial herbs with small, crowded flowers. There are usually 5 sepals and no petals. Filaments of the stamens are often united into a short tube. Familiar examples of this family include the cockscomb (*Celosia*) and the common pigweed (*Amaranthus*).

Froelichia gracilis
Slender Snakecotton

The slender snakecotton grows 1–2 feet high and is unbranched except for the flower stems. These are covered with soft, minute hairs. The flowers, also, are almost covered with these woolly hairs, so that in some cases only the end of the flower is visible, though this might not be apparent without a magnifying glass. They have no petals, but the black-tipped white bracts give the flower head a black-and-white appearance. The flower head, or cluster, ½–1½ inches long, is sometimes attached directly to the stem, but more often grows on a flower stem ½–5 inches long. The slender leaves are at the base of the plant. This one was photographed in the lower elevations of the Davis Mountains in August. *Plains and rocky slopes of West Texas. July–September.*

AMARYLLIDACEAE
Amaryllis or Daffodil Family

The Amaryllis Family resembles the Lily Family in many respects. In both, the flowers are radially symmetrical with 6 tepals and 6 stamens. The principal difference is that the ovary is inferior in some Amaryllidaceae. The leaves arise from a bulb.

In East and Southeast Texas the rain lily, swamp lily, and spider lily are common. In Southwest Texas the genus *Agave* is the most numerous. Some botanists consider this genus as a separate family, the Agavaceae.

Agave lechuguilla
Lechuguilla

The lechuguilla is a common plant of the Chihuahuan desert and is considered one of the principal indicators of the region. Sometimes it covers the ground so thickly one cannot walk through it, and horses are often disabled by the stiff, erect, needle-tipped leaves, which injure their legs and make them lame. Horses familiar with the country can usually avoid it.

The plant reproduces by putting out off-shoots, which are often eaten by deer and javelinas. Human use is also heavy, as rope, mats, and baskets are made from the fiber, while pulque, mescal, and tequila are made from the fermented sap of the flower stalk.

The lechuguilla, like its relative, the maguey or century plant, requires 12–15 years to store up enough food for the production of the large flower stalk, which then grows amazingly fast up to 15 feet tall. The stalk is unbranched and flexible, so that it often bends when it is heavy with buds or flowers, retaining a permanent, graceful arc. The upper part of the stalk is covered with a solid mass of purplish or yellowish flowers. After producing flowers and seeds, the stalk dies.

Photographed in Big Bend National Park in April. *Trans-Pecos. Blooms according to rainfall. Perennial.*

Agave scabra (A. havardiana)
Century Plant (Maguey, Mescal)

This stately sentinel of the Chihuahuan desert is confined almost entirely to that area. It is commonly called the century plant because it takes so long for it to produce a blossom, though under favorable conditions it may be only 12–15 years.

For most of its life the plant is a rosette of thick, fleshy leaves, 1½–2½ feet long, with spines along the margins, including one at the end of each leaf that is longer and stronger than the rest. If this terminal spine is pulled out after the leaf is cut, 2 strong fibers from the outer edge will come out with it, and it can be used for sewing, like a threaded needle. The leaves have many fibers that can be dried, after the pulp is removed, and used in making rope. Three intoxicating beverages—pulque, mescal, and tequila—are made from the sap and sold commercially.

The century plant is most impressive in its flowering stage, when from the center of the rosette a stalk, 4–6 inches in diameter and similar in appearance to asparagus, grows rapidly to a height of 12–20 feet, sometimes growing as much as 18 inches a day. From the upper third of this stalk grow stout stems 1½–3 feet long, each ending in an upturned cluster (6–12 inches in diameter) of yellow tubular flowers. These flower clusters provide a veritable feast for many species of birds, butterflies, and other insects. One was a focal point of interest as we camped near it for several days while it was in bloom. Photographed in the Big Bend National Park in September. *Chihuahuan desert. Spring. Perennial.*

Cooperia pedunculata
Rain Lily

Rain lilies pop up and bloom two or three days after good rains in the spring and early summer. They begin to open slowly about dusk and are fully opened the next morning. Flowers are trumpet-shaped for a few hours after opening, but the 3 petals and 3 sepals, all white, spread widely to 2 inches across as they mature; they last only a day or two. The fragrant blossom is at the top of the single, unbranched stem, which is 5–9 inches high. The leaves are at the bottom, 6–12 inches long and ¼ inch wide. We have seen hundreds of thousands of rain lilies blooming between Luling and Goliad in late April. This one was photographed in McKinney Falls State Park, near Austin, in April. *East, Central, and South Texas. April–September.*

———————————————

Another species, *Cooperia drummondii,* is quite similar, but slightly smaller in every respect. *Throughout the Trans-Pecos and over much of Central and East Texas. April–September.*

Crinum americanum
Swamp Lily (Southern Swamp Lily, String Lily)

Swamp lilies are erect plants that grow in small clumps. The leaves grow directly from the bulb and are 2–4 feet long and 2–3 inches wide. The flower stem is about 1 inch in diameter, 2–3 feet tall, with 2–6 flowers forming a showy umbel at the top. The fragrant flowers are white, sometimes marked with pink. The tepals are 3–4 inches long and ½ inch wide. They are joined at the base, forming a long tube, but curve backward at the end to form a ball-shaped blossom. The upper half of the stamens is purple, with purple anthers extending out from the blossom as the tepals curve backward. We photographed this specimen near Caddo Lake, in July. *Common in freshwater marshes and cypress swamps in Southeast Texas; extends to Northeast Texas, where it is rarer. May–November. Perennial.*

Hymenocallis liriosme
Spider Lily

An elegant and unusual-looking flower,
the spider lily has a stem 1–3 feet
high,with 2 or 3 blossoms at the top. The
flower has 3 white sepals and 3 petals,
which are alike and unite to form a tube
2–4 inches long, narrow but spreading,
and curving backward slightly as they age.
The flowers are quite fragrant. The glossy
leaves, at the base of the plant, are 6–30
inches long and 1 inch wide. Photographed
near Sour Lake, in April. *Found in large
numbers along roadside ditches and
around the edges of swamps or ponds;
particularly abundant along the coast and
in the Big Thicket. March–May. Perennial.*

ANACARDIACEAE
Sumac or Cashew Family

The Sumac Family consists of shrubs, small trees, and woody vines, often with resinous or milky, acrid juice. Leaves are alternate, sometimes simple, often pinnately compound. Leaflets are lobed, entire, or toothed. Flowers are small and numerous on upright panicles. There are usually 5 sepals, separated or united at the base; 5 petals, white to yellow or green; 5 stamens; and 1 pistil.

Rhus glabra
Smooth Sumac

It is the fruit of the smooth sumac, not the flowers, that catches one's eye. This shrub is usually 5–10 feet tall, sometimes taller. The compound leaves are alternate, with 13–30 sharp-toothed leaflets on each side of the midrib. The small flowers grow in branched, pointed, upright clusters, 6–9 inches long, at the end of a stout stem. Each flower has 5 greenish-yellow petals. The flowers are followed by reddish-brown seeds which are a favorite bird food. The seeds remain firmly attached for a long time without noticeable deterioration and are often used in large decorative arrangements. This photo was taken east of Mineola in August. *Open woods, uncultivated fields and pastures, and fencerows in the eastern third of the state. Blooms June–July, depending on growing conditions; fruits late June–August. Perennial.*

Another species, *R. vernix*, is poisonous but can easily be distinguished by its white seeds. It is found only in one small area of Texas, in Shelby County, near the Louisiana line.

Rhus virens
Evergreen Sumac

Evergreen sumac is a shrub 4–8 feet tall with spreading branches. The lower ones sometimes touch the ground. Leaves are alternate, 2–5½ inches long, with 5–9 fleshy leaflets on stiff stems. The upper surface is dark green and shiny but turns red, yellow, or brown in the fall. The 5-petaled, inconspicuous, greenish or white flowers grow in clusters 1–2 inches long at the end of stout branches. When the fruit matures in mid-September it is red, broader than long, and covered with fine hair. Photographed in the Chisos Mountains. *Central and West Texas at altitudes of 2,000–7,500 feet. Blooms irregularly in summer after rains. Perennial.*

APOCYNACEAE
Dogbane or Oleander Family

The stem of the dogbanes, when broken, oozes a bitter sap that keeps grazing animals away; but it lures certain butterflies which, in turn, can secrete a similar bitter substance for protection against their enemies. Leaves are simple, margins entire. Flowers have 5 sepals, 5 petal-like lobes, 2 pistils, and 5 stamens attached to the corolla and alternating with the lobes. The petal-like lobes are joined to form a tube. The cultivated oleander (*Nerium oleander*) belongs to this family.

Amsonia ciliata
Blue Star

The blue star plant grows 15–24 inches tall. The leaves are borne singly, but very close together all the way up the stem to the flower cluster. They are ½ inch wide and 2 inches long, with one vein running lengthwise down the center and attached directly to the main stem (without a petiole). The leaves are smooth, soft, and slightly smaller toward the upper part of the stem. The narrow tube of the pale blue flower, ½ inch long, opens into 5 petal-like lobes in a star shape ½ inch across, with a ring of white at the center. Several blossoms grow in a loose cluster at the tips of the stems. This one was photographed on the YO Ranch, near Mountain Home, growing in a clump of bear grass, in April. *Central Texas. April–June. Perennial.*

Macrosiphonia macrosiphon
Longtube Trumpet Flower

This plant is 6–12 inches tall. The leaves
grow close together on the stem. On some
plants, they are almost round with broad
scallops; on others they have entire margins with a point at the tip. All of them
are fleshy with a covering of fine hair on
both sides and prominent veins and midrib. A single flower grows at the end of a
stem. The flower tube is 2–5 inches long,
gradually spreading to 5 creamy-white,
petal-like lobes; the whole flower is about
1½ inches across. We photographed this
one in the Davis Mountains in August.
South-Central and West Texas. June–
September.

ARACEAE
Arum or Calla Family

Members of the Arum Family have three outstanding features: (1) They grow in wet ground. (2) The individual flowers are minute, having no petals or sepals, though some may have small scales. The tiny flowers are grouped closely on a fleshy spike (spadix), with male flowers on the upper part and female flowers on the lower part. (3) The spike is thumblike in shape, always wrapped in a leaf-like sheathing called a spathe. It may be brightly colored and resemble a petal.

This family is extensively represented in the Tropics, where it includes many vines and tree-like plants. Those found in Texas are all herbaceous. The most familiar is the jack-in-the-pulpit.

Arisaema dracontium
Green Dragon (Dragonroot)

Green Dragon has only 1 leaf; however, the leaf stem forks so that there appear to be 2 separate leaves, each divided into 5–15 unequal leaflets which are arranged palmately (like the upturned palm of one's hand) on the tip of the forked stem, which is sometimes 20 inches long. There are numerous tiny flowers crowded onto the 6-inch-long flower stem, the lower part of which is enclosed within the leaf stem. The white flowers are very small, with no petals or sepals. This one was photographed on the banks of Cow Creek, south of Burkeville, in May. *Southeast Texas. May–June. Perennial.*

ASCLEPIADACEAE
Milkweed Family

The Milkweed Family gets its name from the thick white sap that oozes from any broken surface of most of the species (although this is true of certain other families also). Many species attract butterflies. The flowers are usually in umbels of very small flowers that range from greenish white to dull pink to orange-red. The 5-lobed corolla is united. Leaves are usually paired. The unusual structure of the flower makes it distinctive. The tips of the 5 stamens are joined with a broad disc which is supported by the 2 styles of the pistil, forming a petal-like crown. The boat-shaped pods contain seeds tufted with silky hairs.

Arisaema quinatum
**Five-leaved Jack-in-the-Pulpit
(Indian Turnip)**

There are two species of jack-in-the-pulpit in East Texas, both 1–2 feet tall and very similar, except that this one has 5 leaflets forming the leaf and the other, *A. triphyllum*, has 3. Flowers grow on a long, thick spike that is enclosed by a fleshy bract (in this case an enlarged leaf) with a flap over the top. It has the general likeness of an old-fashioned pulpit with a canopy over it, which suggests its common name. The many tiny flowers are off-white in color. It has pistillate flowers at the base and staminate flowers in the middle portion. This one was photographed near Burkeville in May. *East Texas. April–June. Perennial.*

Asclepias asperula
Green-flowered Milkweed

The green-flowered milkweed grows 1–2
feet tall, with spreading stems that form
large, dense clumps. The leaves are 4–
8 inches long, narrow, and irregularly
grouped. Stems are densely covered with
minute hairs. The flowers are crowded
into a ball-shaped head, 3–4 inches across,
at the end of the flower stem and are intri-
cately arranged. Inside the partially divided petals is a crown, out of which
extend 5 white stamens with large, ball-
like anthers, all symmetrically arranged.
Photographed on Jim Bowmer's ranch,
near Temple. *Dry, sandy, or rocky places
in Northeast and Central Texas. March–
October. Perennial.*

BERBERIDACEAE
Barberry Family

The Barberry Family contains both shrubs and herbaceous plants. Most members of this family have alternate leaves, the mayapple being an exception. Sepals and petals are usually in 2 rows of 3 each. There are as many stamens as petals (or twice as many, in the case of the mayapple), and a single pistil.

Asclepias tuberosa
Butterfly Weed (Orange Milkweed)

The leaves of the butterfly weed are poisonous to livestock, but many butterflies, especially the Monarch, feed on the nectar. We have seen up to 4 different species of butterflies on a small plant at once.

The plant grows 1–2 feet tall. It is difficult to transplant because of the long taproot. The leaves are mostly alternate, 1½–2¼ inches long, pointed, and smooth on the edge. The yellow-orange to bright-orange flower clusters, 2–5 inches across, are at the top of the flowering stem. Photographed near Tyler in June. *Sandy areas of East and Central Texas. May–July. Perennial.*

— — — — — — — — — — — —

In the Davis Mountains another milkweed, *A. latifolia*, grows 2–3 feet tall, with no branches but numerous large leaves, 3–4 inches long and 2 inches wide. They are attached directly to the main stem and are coarse with prominent veins. The pale green to yellowish flowers are almost hidden by the leaves. *Grasslands between Alpine and Fort Davis and in the lower part of the mountains. July–October. Perennial.*

Berberis trifoliolata (Mahonia trifolio-lata)
Agarita (Algerita, Wild Currant, Laredo Mahonia)

Agarita is an evergreen shrub, 3–10 feet tall, with stiff, spiny, holly-like leaves. They are alternate, 2–4 inches long, divided into three leaflets which have 3–7 lobes ending in sharp spines. The yellow flowers have 6 petals and 6 sepals, which are similar, forming a cup shape around the stamens and pistils. They are an important source of nectar for bees, and the roots furnish a yellow dye used by early pioneers. The lustrous red fruit, is a pea-sized berry that is used in making jelly and wine. It is also a choice food for many birds. We photographed this agarita on Adam Wilson's ranch at the north end of Sabinal Canyon, in March. *Dry, stony soil over most of Texas except east and southeast portions. Blooms February–April; fruits mainly in June. Perennial.*

Podophyllum peltatum
Mayapple (Mandrake)

The erect, 1-stemmed mayapple plant grows to 20 inches tall. It has only 2 leaves and 1 flower, which grows in the axil of the leaves. The petiole is attached to the lower surface of the leaf near the center, and the thin, light-green leaves are deeply lobed. The flower is covered by the 2 large, umbrella-shaped leaves, which are 6–8 inches across; it can be seen only from the side. It is 2 inches in diameter and has 6–9 waxy white petals, with many stamens.

The mayapple tends to form colonies from creeping, underground stems and thick, fibrous roots. This one was photographed in Caddo Lake State Park, near Jefferson, in April. *Abundant in the damp woods of East Texas. March–April. Perennial.*

BIGNONIACEAE
Catalpa Family

Members of the Catalpa Family include trees, shrubs, and woody vines. Leaves are opposite (uppermost leaves may sometimes be alternate), simple or pinnately compound, entire to toothed or lobed. Flowers are rather large and showy, on terminal branches or spikelike racemes or in the axils, and paired or whorled. The calyx is short and 2-lipped, or unequally 4–5 toothed. Corolla is 2-lipped or nearly regular and 5-lobed. There are 2 or 4 stamens and 1 pistil.

Bignonia capreolata
Crossvine

The evergreen, woody crossvine is easy to locate because of its large, attractive, trumpet-shaped flowers, 2 inches long and 1½ inches across, deep red on the outside and red to yellowish on the inside. The flowers grow in clusters of 4 to 6. They are sometimes seen high in a tree, as the vine climbs by means of tendrils. Leaves are opposite, 4–6 inches long by 2 inches wide, with a third leaflet modified into a tendril. Surprisingly, the odor of the flowers is unpleasant. This specimen was photographed near Saratoga in April. *Grows over most of East Texas; sometimes cultivated. April–June. Perennial.*

Campsis radicans
Common Trumpet Creeper (Cow Vine, Foxglove Vine)

Trumpet creeper is a woody vine, climbing tall trees by means of aerial rootlets, or sometimes creeping on the ground. Leaves are opposite, 8–15 inches long, with 7–13 leaflets, coarsely toothed, ¾–3 inches long and ½–2 inches wide, olive green and shiny above. It blooms all summer over all of East Texas, and less frequently as far west as Austin and San Antonio. It has 2–9 orange-red blossoms in a cluster. They are trumpet-shaped, 2–3½ inches long, opening into 5 petal-like lobes. The plant is frequently cultivated because of its large clusters of attractive, bright red flowers, and its appeal to hummingbirds. It is pollinated by them and by long-tongued bees. It is a hardy plant and, unless controlled, can become a pest. Photographed near Lake Tyler in June. *East to Central Texas. June–September. Perennial.*

Catalpa bignonioides
Southern Catalpa (Cigar Tree)

The catalpa grows to 40 feet tall and has many branches. Its heart-shaped leaves have prominent veins and are 6–12 inches long and half as wide. The petiole is almost as long as the leaf. The flowers are in clusters of 10–20, each blossom on a short stem. They are white, 2-lipped, united at the base, opening into 5 ruffled, petal-like lobes; each flower is about 2 inches across. In the throat there are 2 large yellow spots and several smaller ones, several small purple stripes, and a number of tiny purple spots. The tree is cultivated as an ornamental but has long since escaped cultivation. Photographed in May on Peggy Foster's place in Saratoga. *Varied habitats throughout East Texas. April–May. Perennial.*

Chilopsis linearis
Desert Willow (Flowering Willow, Willow-leaved Catalpa)

This willow-like shrub grows 6–10 feet tall as a rule, but occasionally higher. Leaves are deciduous, both opposite and alternate, 4–12 inches long and ⅓ inch wide. When not in flower it might go unnoticed among the heavier growth of shrubs along the banks of arroyos or in the mountains; but its beautiful orchid-like flowers of white to purple make it an eyecatcher. The blossom is funnel-shaped, 1–1½ inches long, spreading at the opening into 5 ruffled, petal-like lobes. The flower is dark pink or purple, often with white or yellow and purple streakings within the throat. By early autumn the violet-scented flowers, which appear after summer rains, are replaced by slender seedpods, 6–10 inches long, which remain dangling from the branches and serve to identify the tree after the flowers are gone. This tree was photographed in the Chisos Mountains at 6,000 feet in July. *Common in the Trans-Pecos below 4,000 feet; abundant at higher elevations in the Chisos and Davis mountains. April–September (mostly May–June). Perennial.*

Tecoma stans
Yellow Trumpet Flower (Yellow Bells)

This shrub is 2–5 feet tall with several branches in the upper part. Leaves are opposite, 4–8 inches long, with 7–9 narrow leaflets, 1½–4 inches long, sharply toothed, and shiny. The yellow, trumpet-shaped flowers are 1¼–1¾ inches long and up to 2 inches across. Flowers are in a long cluster at the top of the stems. This plant would be suitable for cultivation, as it has a showy flower with a long blooming period. Photographed in the Davis Mountains in July. *Trans-Pecos, west to the Davis Mountains. May–October. Perennial.*

BORAGINACEAE
Borage or Forget-Me-Not Family

The genera in this family are almost all characterized by blossoms consisting of 1-sided cymes, usually tightly coiled and uncoiling as the fruits develop. Flowers have a 5-lobed corolla with 5 stamens. The petals form a funnel or tube, with lobes at right angles. Most of the plants are rough and hairy, with simple, alternate leaves.

Heliotropium indicum
Turnsole

Turnsole is a coarse plant, 2 feet tall or sometimes higher. Leaves are alternate and conspicuously veined, usually 6 inches long and 4 inches wide, somewhat crimped. Flowers are blue or violet, very small but numerous, in 2 rows on the upper side of a curved spike 4–12 inches long. The spike straightens out as the flowers open. This one was photographed in the Big Thicket, near Saratoga, in September. *East and South Texas. June–October. Annual.*
— — — — — — — — — —
The blossoms of *Cryptantha coryi*, a similar plant in the same family, also grow on the upper side of a curved stem which straightens as the seeds form. The small white flowers, about ¼ inch across, turn pinkish as they mature. The narrow leaves, 1½–2 inches long, are slightly wider toward the tip. The plant grows 8–12 inches tall, usually unbranched. Stem and leaves are covered with rough gray hairs. *In gravelly soil from Del Rio to the Big Bend area. April–August.*

Lithospermum incisum
Puccoon (Narrowleaf Gromwell, Golden Puccoon)

The puccoon is found in fields and on roadsides throughout the state but grows best in sandy soils in the eastern half. Leaves are alternate, 2–4 inches long with rolled edges, larger near the base. Flowers are often in clusters at the end of stems which are 6–12 inches long. They are trumpet-shaped with 5 petal-like lobes which open to 1 inch across, with crinkled margins. This specimen was photographed west of Palestine in June, but we have also photographed puccoon in the Davis Mountains in West Texas. *Statewide. March–July. Perennial.*

— — — — — — — — — — — — — —

Another attractive flower in this genus is *L. multiflorum*, widespread in the mountains above 4,000 feet. It is 9–18 inches tall and has basal leaves smaller than those above, a reversal of the general rule. Leaves are alternate and close together on the stem; the upper leaves are 1–2 inches long, narrow and blunt. The upper half is branched, with a compact cluster of flowers at the tip of the stem, ½–¾ inch long, with 5 round, yellow petals 1¼ inches across. *West Texas. June–October.*

CACTACEAE
Cactus Family

A unique feature of the Cactus Family is the structure called the areole, a brown or blackish spot, up to ½ inch across, from which spines grow in clusters. These are usually arranged in rows or spirals on the pads or stems, and are found on stem projections called tubercles.

Cacti are succulents, which store large amounts of water in their tissues and can withstand long periods of drought. The waxy surface of the stems, or pads, retards evaporation and conserves moisture. The thick spines discourage animals from feeding on them and also serve to shade the surface.

The flowers are radially symmetrical, with 5 or more sepals and many thin petals. Often petals and sepals are indistinguishable and grade into each other, joining at the base into a floral tube of varying length. Flowers have numerous stamens, a single style, and several stigmas. The ovary is inferior.

Cacti produce some of our most beautiful wildflowers, and the brightly colored fruit of many species is edible. There are about 75 species in Texas, with wide variation in size.

Echinocactus texensis
Horse Crippler (Devil's Head)

The horse crippler cactus is broader than it is long. Normally it is 1–2 inches above the ground and up to 12 inches across. It is difficult to see, and many horses have been crippled from stepping on it. It usually has only 1 stem, occasionally 2 or 3. If injured at the tip, it may produce a cluster of small heads on top of the old one. The surface of the plant is dark green. It has about 14 spines at each areole, with a central spine that is longer and stronger than the others, 2–3 inches long and straight to slightly curved downward. The inverted bell-shaped flowers are 1–2¾ inches across and about as tall. The outer petals are salmon-red, the inner ones salmon-pink with streaks of red. The edge of the petals has a feathery appearance. Anthers are pinkish to red, and the pistil is yellow to pink. The flower is somewhat fragrant. We photographed this plant 2 miles west of Tivoli, in April. *Found over most of the state west of a line from Matagorda to Fort Worth and Wichita Falls, and south of the Panhandle. Blooms April–May (peak times) but sometimes earlier or later depending on moisture and temperature. Perennial.*

Echinocereus chisoensis
Chisos Hedgehog

Chisos hedgehogs grow to 8 inches tall, but seldom more than 2 inches in diameter. They are usually single, but branch out occasionally above the ground. Each plant has 13–16 ribs composed of quite distinct tubercles, almost completely separated from each other by broad valleys. The surface is bluish-green to deep green. There are ten to fifteen spines growing from each areole, most of which lie flat on the stem. The flowers are about 2½ inches long and 1–2 inches across and never open wide. The base of the petals is deep red followed by a pinkish-white band, with the upper portion pink to rose colored. Stamens are cream-colored, and the pistil has several green lobes. This rare hedgehog grows only in the Chisos Mountains, where we photographed it in April. *Perennial.*

Echinocereus enneacanthus
Strawberry Cactus (Pitaya)

The cylindrical stems of the strawberry cactus are 3–30 inches long and 1½–4 inches in diameter. They grow in loose clusters of a few to as many as 100. New stems grow as side branches, near the ground, so their first growth tends to be lateral, later turning upward, giving them a long, curling appearance. There are 7–10 ribs on each stem. The plant is bright green with a wrinkled appearance, looking withered in dry periods. The stems are often yellow-green in sunny locations. The tubercles are about ⅛ inch in diameter and ¼–1½ inches apart on mature stems. This cactus has fewer spines and shows more plant surface than most cacti.

The purplish-red flowers are 2–3 inches long and about the same in diameter. They have 10–20 outer petals with pinkish, crinkled edges. The inner petals, 12–35, are in 1–3 rows. Anthers on the stamens are yellow, and the pistil has 8–12 lobes like most other *Echinocereus.* The fruit is about 1 inch long, almost round, greenish to brown or purple.

The specimen shown here, the largest we have ever seen, was 6 feet across, due to its favorable location. We found it grow-ing under a mesquite tree near the Rio Grande, 20 miles west of Terlingua, where it was helped along by a seep in the hillside rocks that gave it extra moisture. Since it was shaded, most of the flowers bloomed at the same time, creating an unusual floral display.

Found along the Rio Grande almost from its mouth to Big Bend National Park. Blooms most profusely in April. Perennial.

————————————————

E. stramineus or pitaya has many large spines that distinguish it from *E. enneacanthus,* which often shares the same habitat. It has 11–13 ribs with fairly deep furrows between them. They tend to cluster, sometimes forming large, compact clumps with 100 or more stems. These larger clumps are rounded, often 2–3 feet across and nearly as high. Stems are about 10 inches tall and 3½ inches in diameter. The purple-red flowers are 4–5 inches tall and 3–4 inches across. They are dark red at the base, fading to rose at the tips. The inner petals are toothed. The 10–15 outer petals have pink edges.

Echinocereus pectinatus var.
neomexicanus
**Texas Rainbow Cactus (Golden
Rainbow Hedgehog)**

The Texas rainbow cactus is oval at first,
soon becoming cylindrical, and grows to
15 inches or so, with a 4-inch diameter.
The stems commonly remain single, but
old plants sometimes branch and form
several heads. Each head has 12–21 narrow
ribs. Fifteen to 25 spines grow out of the
areoles, spreading widely and intertwining
with those of other areoles. Flowers are
about 3–6 inches long and are pale yellow to orange. Petals are quite long and
pointed. Outer petals are sometimes
tinged with magenta on the outside, and
inner petals are streaked with green on the
inside. The base of the petals is green. The
stamens are cream-colored. Photographed
east of Tornillo Creek, near Rio Grande
Village, in late March. *Grows widely over
Central and West Texas. March–May.
Perennial.*

Echinocereus reichenbachii
Lace Cactus (Purple Candle)

Like other cylindrical cacti, lace cactus
starts out as a sphere and gradually
evolves its cylindrical form as it matures. This little plant rarely grows taller
than 8 inches and is 2–3 inches across. It
is unpredictable in its development, one
plant forming a single stem, while its
neighbor may branch out and form a
dozen or more. It has 10–20 narrow ribs.
The outer spines vary from 12 to 36 and
are flattened against the stem. The central
spines vary from none to 6 and project
outward.

The flowers are brilliant purple or rose-
pink, 2–5 inches tall and almost as wide.
There are 30–50 petals with ragged edges,
sometimes notched. The base of the petals
is usually reddish-brown. Stamens are
cream-colored to yellow, and the pistil has
many dark-green lobes, varying in number
with each flower. Photographed near Men-
ard in April. *From South-Central Texas,
northwest throughout the Panhandle
April–May. Perennial.*

Echinocereus triglochidiatus
Claret Cup Cactus (Hedgehog Cactus)

One of the most attractive hedgehog cacti is the claret cup, which grows in clumps as much as 3–4 feet across but usually smaller. The bright red-orange flowers often cover the whole plant, which is cylindrical and low-growing, often hugging up against some larger plant. The numerous flowers grow at the top of the stems, all about the same height, giving a full view of all the flowers at one glance. They last for several days. The flowers vary slightly in color as a result of soil type or genetic differences. Photographed in the Chisos Mountains, Big Bend National Park, just off the South Rim Trail, in the "Meadow," in April. *From Del Rio throughout the Trans-Pecos. April–May. Perennial.*

Echinocereus russanthus
Rusty Hedgehog Cactus

E. *russanthus* is heavily covered with a mass of interlocking bristlelike, slender spines radiating in all directions. It grows to 10 inches tall and 2–3 inches in diameter. The stems often branch and form clusters, some having as many as a dozen. Each has 13–18 ribs. Flowers are rust-red with darker lines, about 1 inch long and 1 inch across.

It grows from the Chisos Mountains in Big Bend National Park northwest to Study Butte. This one was photographed northwest of the Chisos, north of the road from Park Headquarters to Terlingua, in April. *Far West Texas. April–May. Perennial.*

Ferocactus hamatacanthus
Turk's Head

In its early stages of growth the Turk's head is rather round, but it becomes columnar as it reaches maturity, about 8 inches tall and 8 inches in diameter. It usually has a single stem but occasionally will branch. It has 13–17 large, broad ribs with tubercles up to 2 inches high. Out of the tubercles grow 8–14 outer spines and 4–8 central ones, the lowest of which is extremely long, up to 6 inches, and hooked on the end.

Echinocereus viridiflorus var. *cylindricus*
Green-flowered Hedgehog

The green-flowered hedgehog cactus grows singly, never in clusters or mounds, and is sometimes as much as 3 inches in diameter and 8 inches tall. The flowers are about 1 inch long and 1 inch broad, smaller than others in this genus. They vary from yellowish-green to brownish, and grow well down on the sides, often forming a band around the middle. The fruit is small and spiny. Photographed in the Davis Mountains in July. *Blooms in the mountains of West Texas. April–May (peak); later if moisture and temperature are good.*

The flowers are 2½–4 inches tall, almost as wide, and fragrant, though one should be steady on one's feet when smelling them. There are up to 30 inner petals, which are long and wide, but pointed at the tip. They are yellow, sometimes red at the base. The pistils and the anthers are yellow. The pistils extend beyond the stamens. The favored range of this cactus is along the Rio Grande River from the Devils River to El Paso, but we photographed this one in the Davis Mountains State Park, in July. *West Texas. April–July. Perennial.*

Ferocactus uncinatus var. *wrightii*
Brown-flowered Hedgehog (Catclaw Cactus)

This hedgehog is oval shaped, up to 8 inches tall and 4 inches across but usually much smaller. It has 13 high, conspicuous ribs, separated by broad grooves. The surface is bluish-green. There are 7 or 8 heavy spines at each areole. The upper 4 are straight and flattened, about 1–2 inches long, but the lower ones are somewhat shorter and nearly round, curved at the tips. There is 1 central spine, 2–4 inches long, very heavy, and often twisted and hooked at the tip. Flowers are maroon to reddish-brown, funnel-shaped, up to 1¼ inches long and about 1 inch across. The petals are sometimes slightly pointed at the tip; others are squared off. The pistil is brown, with 19 or more broad lobes which are cream-colored above and maroon below. Stamens are yellow. Photographed west of Presidio in April. *Grows from the east side of Big Bend National Park north to Marathon and northwest to El Paso. April–May. Perennial.*

Ferocactus wislizeni
Fishhook Barrel Cactus (Candy Barrel)

The fishhook barrel cactus is one of our rarest cacti, and the largest. Its range in Texas is confined to the far west. It is round in its early stages, then oval or cone-shaped, and finally cylindrical. It grows to 4 feet tall or more, and about 2 feet across. It has 13–25 vertical ribs extending from the bottom to the top of the stem. The tubercles that make up the ribs are pointed. The yellowish-red or purplish-red spines are in groups of 12–20, with 3 or 4 much stronger than the others, 1½–4 inches long. The upper 3 are straight, and the fourth is usually hooked downward and is much heavier than the other 3. The flowers vary in color among shades of yellow, gold, red, and orange, and are about 2 inches long and up to 3 inches across. The petals are short in relation to the width of the center portion. This specimen was photographed in the Franklin Mountains near El Paso in April.

Neolloydia conoidea
Cone Cactus

This small, low-growing cactus is egg-shaped at first, later becoming cone-like, about 4 inches tall and almost 3 inches across. It often sprouts near the base, or even higher on the sides, to produce 2 or 3 branches. The surface is dull green and has several rows of pyramid-shaped tubercles about ½ inch high. There are 10–16 spines that are straight, rigid, and radiate outward, lying flat on the stem, and 1–4 spines in the center, ⅜–1 inch long, that project outward. These are black when young, fading to gray. The flowers are violet or violet-pink, 1–2 inches across, about 1 inch deep, and opening out widely. The petals are long and pointed and the stamens are yellow-orange. The fruit is round, yellowish or reddish, later turning brown. This one was photographed about 40 miles west of Del Rio in September, much later than its usual blooming period. *Confined primarily to the area between Del Rio and Boquillas. April–June (peak). Perennial.*

Opuntia grahamii
Graham Dog Cactus

The Graham dog cactus often forms low mounds with many branches. The last joint on the branches is erect and widest near the top, about 2 inches long or less. It has rough, wartlike structures on the joints, giving the plant a rough, dull appearance, an unlikely place to find the attractive yellow flowers it produces. The flowers open in the early afternoon. The joints of this plant, like those of other chollas, break off easily and hang on to anything that barely touches them. Photographed in the Big Bend in April. *Widely scattered over the Trans-Pecos. March–July. Perennial.*

Opuntia humifusa
Low Prickly Pear (Smooth Prickly Pear)

This low-growing prickly pear is the most widespread of all of the cacti in the United States and is found all over Texas. It seldom grows higher than 14 inches, as the pads tend to lie on the ground. It has relatively few or no large spines. This is a characteristic which distinguishes the genus *Opuntia* from other genera in the United States. The flowers are quite attractive, 2–5 inches across, pale yellow to orange-yellow, or orange-yellow with red centers. The 4–9 pistils are whitish to yellow, and the anthers are cream-colored. This one was photographed west of Canton in May. *Statewide. March–July. Perennial.*

Opuntia imbricata
Cholla (Cane Cactus)

An unusual cholla that frequently grows to 8 feet tall, sometimes even more, *O. imbricata* is an eyecatcher when in bloom. It is often found along fencerows, but also forms thickets in open areas. The cylindrical joints grow in any and every direction, giving it an unpredictable and sometimes grotesque shape. The joints are round and are almost covered with small, uniform growth structures that give them an interesting texture. The magenta-purplish-red flowers are about 3 inches across. The yellow fruit at the end of the joints ripens in August and stays on the plant through the winter months. Since the fruit is free of spines, it is often eaten by deer and cattle. The dead stems of this cholla, with holes at odd angles all along the stem, are used for lamp stands and all sorts of handicraft items. Photographed near Fort Stockton in June. *Throughout the Trans-Pecos. April–June. Perennial.*

Opuntia leptocaulis
Tasajillo (Christmas Cactus)

Tasajillo gets its English name, Christmas cactus, from the bright red fruit it produces, which is as beautiful as its 1-inch greenish-yellow blossoms. Stems are from pencil size to 1 inch in diameter. The fruit is a favorite food of quail, which accounts for the fact that many plants are found along fencerows (where seeds come up from the droppings of the birds). Tasajillo often forms thickets in the Big Bend country. We have photographed it from San Antonio to the Davis Mountains; this photo was taken between Marble Falls and Kingsland in April. *Spread widely over Central and West Texas. April–July. Perennial.*

Opuntia lindheimeri
Texas Prickly Pear

Texas prickly pear often grows to 5 feet tall. It may be erect or spreading, with a more or less definite trunk. The pads are green to blue-green, round to oval, 4–10 inches long. The tubercles are 1½–2½ inches apart. The 1–6 spines are yellow, which distinguishes this species from *O. phaeacantha* varieties. One spine is longer than the rest, about 4½ inches. Occasionally a plant is spineless. The flowers, 2–5 inches across, are often crowded on the edge of the pad. They have several greenish-yellow sepals. Petals vary from yellow to yellow-orange to red, often with the whole range of colors on one plant. Flowers have 1 pistil and many yellow stamens. The fruit is a prickly pear, maturing purple, very seedy. Photographed near Cotulla in April. *South, Southwest, and Central Texas. Mostly April–May. Perennial.*

Opuntia phaeacantha var. *discata*
Prickly Pear

This is perhaps the most abundant prickly
pear in West Texas, and one of the most
attractive. The masses of yellow to orange
flowers it produces will bring one to a
stop, no matter how often they are en-
countered. The plant itself is sometimes
8 feet across and almost as tall. The fruits,
called "tuna," are up to 2½ inches long,
with a deep maroon color that makes the
plant attractive after the flowers are gone.
They are edible, but have too many seeds
to be enjoyed. I once sucked the juice from
a dozen of them when very thirsty, and,
although it helped, I recommend better attention to one's water supply. Photographed in Big Bend National Park in
April. *West Texas. April–May. Perennial.*

Opuntia phaeacantha var. *major*
Brown-spined Prickly Pear (New Mexico Prickly Pear)

The brown-spined prickly pear has flowers that are 2–3 inches across, bright yellow, with red to maroon centers. The stamens are yellowish or cream-colored, and the pistil is white to pinkish. The plant sometimes grows 2–3 feet tall, occasionally even higher, with no trunk, and forms dense thickets up to 8 feet across; or it may remain a low, prostrate plant with most of the pads resting their edges on the ground, never growing higher than 18 inches. The pads vary widely. Most of them are flat, but others are egg-shaped or club-shaped, 4–9 inches long and 3–7 inches wide. The surface is bluish-green when young, becoming yellowish-green as it grows older. The areoles are ¾–1 inch apart. This one was photographed east of Tornillo Creek, in Big Bend National Park, in April. *Western half of state. April–May. Perennial.*

Opuntia rufida
Blind Prickly Pear

Blind prickly pear has an obvious trunk, with many branches, and grows to 5 feet tall. Its joints are circular, dull gray-green, and the pads are covered with many short brown spines. The flowers are about 3 inches across, yellow to bright red-orange, with the full range of colors visible on the same plant at the same time. The fruit is about 1 inch long. This one was photographed in the Christmas Mountains in April. *Big Bend area. March–July. Perennial.*

Opuntia violaceae var. *macrocentra*
Purple Prickly Pear

The stems of the purple prickly pear are upright, 2–3 feet tall, but without the trunklike main stem. The pads are 4–8 inches long, usually about ½ inch thick. Sometimes they are green, but more often they are purplish overall, especially in the winter and in dry, hot summers. The areoles are about ½ inch apart on small plants, but up to 1¼ inches apart on large ones. The flowers are about 3 inches in diameter, light yellowish with red centers. The anthers are yellow. The fruit is ¾–1½ inches long, round to oval, becoming bright red or orange when ripe. These cacti present a spectacular sight in April, their peak blooming period, with as many as 65–70 large blossoms on one plant. This one was photographed between Terlingua and Study Butte, in April. *From the Big Bend area, northwest through the Davis Mountains, to the Van Horn area. April–May. Perennial.*

The prickly pear was introduced in Eritrea, in northern Ethiopia, to help stop erosion on the mountainsides, and prospered so well on the barren slopes that one could not shoot a rifle at the mountainside without hitting a prickly pear. We were there during the "harvest season," when the girls, boys, men, and women were bringing the fruits into Asmara on camels, burros, bicycles, in boxes on their heads, and every imaginable way. They were sold for making jelly, which was very good.

CAMPANULACEAE
Bluebell or Lobelia Family

In Gray's *Manual of Botany* the lobelias are considered a subfamily of the Bluebell Family. The lobelias are bilaterally symmetrical and 2-lipped while the bluebells are radially symmetrical and bell-shaped or funnel-shaped.

Lobelias found in Texas are characterized by a corolla with 2 small lobes forming the upper lip and 3 larger lobes forming the lower, and by a split in the corolla tube between the 2 upper lobes, extending nearly to the base. The joined stamens form a curved tube which projects upward through the split in the corolla tube.

Most species in this family have alternate, simple leaves. Flowers have 5 petals that are joined, some forming a bell shape, others spreading into a 5-lobed disc. They are generally blue or white and have 5 stamens. The ovary is half or wholly inferior.

Lobelia appendiculata
Pale Lobelia

The slender stem of the pale lobelia is erect, 14–24 inches tall, usually unbranched. The leaves, 1–1½ inches long, are below the spike of flowers. Flowers are pale blue to white, about ⅝ inch long, growing directly on the stem. They are 2-lipped, tubular, and arranged loosely on a spike 6–15 inches long. The lower lip is 3-lobed and longer than the upper, which is 2-lobed and stands up like tufts of feathers above an owl's eyes. This plant was photographed north of Tyler in May. *East Texas. April–August. Annual or biennial.*

— — — — — — — — — — — — — — —

Another beautiful species is *L. fenestralis*, which has purplish, 2-lipped flowers, ½ inch long, crowded on a spike. It grows in West Texas. We found it in Limpia Canyon in the Davis Mountains. *August–October. Annual or biennial.*

Lobelia cardinalis
Cardinal Flower

The beautiful cardinal flower can be found in all parts of the state, from the Chihuahuan desert to the Big Thicket; however, it requires moist areas and thus is more abundant in East Texas. Often cardinal flowers are found along stream banks, just above the water line, where they are worked heavily by the sulphur butterfly. The blossoms are along the top third of the leafy, unbranched stem, 1–4 feet tall. Each scarlet, tubular flower is 1½–2¼ inches long, opening into 5 petal-like lobes, 2-lipped; the upper 2 lobes are longer and narrower than the lower 3. There are 5 stamens with light-gray anthers that contrast sharply with the scarlet-red flower. This plant would make a good addition to one's garden. Photographed in the Big Thicket in September. *Statewide. May–December, depending on location and moisture. Perennial.*

Triodanis perfoliata
Venus' Looking Glass

Venus' looking glass is a stout, erect, unbranched plant, 12–20 inches tall. It is hairy, with longer hairs on the lower side of the leaves, along the veins. Leaves are alternate; those at the base, attached directly to the stem, are broader than long. There are 1 or more flowers in the leaf axils. The early flowers often lack petals and have 3 or 4 short sepals, but later flowers have 5 sepals and 5 bluish-purple petals, united to form a slender tube that flares out nearly flat at the opening. This photo was taken between Bonham and Paris, in May. *Fields and open woods in East and Northeast Texas and west to the Trans-Pecos. April–July. Annual.*

CAPPARIDACEAE
Caper or Spiderflower Family

In most of its floral characteristics, the
Caper Family resembles the mustards.
Flowers are somewhat bilaterally symmetrical, with 4 sepals, 4 petals, and 6 or
more stamens. The alternate leaves are
borne singly on the stem, undivided or divided palmately into 3–7 segments.

Cleome houtteana
Spiderflower

The spiderflower has a sturdy stem 3–6
feet tall. The lower leaves, 3–6 inches
long, are alternate and compound, with
5–7 leaflets. The leaflets grow from a central point, are pointed at both ends, and
are finely toothed. Upper leaves are
abundant but much smaller, about 1½
inches long, and not compound. There is a
dense flower cluster at the top of the stem,
sometimes 1–2 feet long. Flowers are
white, turning pink as they age, ¾–1½
inches long on a flower stem the same
length, with flowers usually on one side of
the stem. The pistil and 6 stamens are
much longer than the petals. This one was
photographed near Tyler in July. *South
and East Texas. April–October. Annual.*

Polanisia uniglandulosa
Clammyweed

Clammyweeds are sticky and strong-smelling. Their upright stems are heavily leafed, each leaf being divided into 3 segments. The flowers are clustered at the end of the stems. The petals are white, erect, ⅝–1⅛ inches long, and notched at the tip. There are as many as 28 stamens, ¾–2 inches long, with purplish anthers. The stamens are longer than the petals, giving the flower a striking deep purple and white effect. Fruit pods are erect, 2–3 inches long. Photographed in the Davis Mountains in August. *Common in West Texas at elevations above 4,000 feet; usually abundant in dry stream beds. May–October.*

Wislizenia refracta
Jackass Clover (Spectacle Fruit)

Jackass clover is a sturdy plant, 3–5 feet tall with many branches. Most of the leaves are divided into 3 segments. The yellow flowers, about ½ inch across, grow in clusters around the upper fourth of the stem and bloom from the bottom up. The many stamens extend beyond the petals and persist even after the petals wither, giving the flower head a feathery appearance. They often grow so thickly that they give a yellow cast to a considerable area. The range of this flower is reported to cover most of Texas, but we have not seen it east of Big Bend National Park. This one was photographed west of Van Horn, in August. *July–October.*

CAPRIFOLIACEAE
Honeysuckle Family

The Honeysuckle Family consists of trees, shrubs, and woody vines, including honeysuckle, elderberries, and arrowwood (*Viburnum dentatum*). Leaves are opposite, with or without petioles, simple or pinnately compound, entire or toothed or lobed. Flowers are in the axils or at the end of flower stems, solitary or in spikes, racemes, umbels, or corymbs. There is a calyx with 3–5 minute to large lobes; a corolla with united petals, 2-lipped or regular, and 5-lobed, funnel-shaped, wheel-shaped, or tubular; 1 pistil, with style and stigma, and usually as many stamens as lobes of the corolla.

Lonicera sempervirens
Coral Honeysuckle (Woodbine)

Coral honeysuckle is a woody, evergreen vine, with runners 15 feet long or longer. There are 1–4 clusters of trumpet-shaped, coral blossoms that surround the stem, with 6–12 blossoms in a cluster. They bloom from the bottom up. The blossoms are a deep red, often yellowish in the throat, with yellow stamens protruding. The upper leaves which encircle the stem of the flower are round to oval, the oval leaves pointed on the ends. They are thick, pale green above and white on the underside. The larger, lower leaves are almost 3 inches long and half as wide, blunt or rounded on the tips. This photograph was made near Tyler in May. *Common in the eastern half of Texas; widely cultivated. March–May. Perennial.*
— — — — — — — — — — — — —
Japanese honeysuckle, *L. japonica*, appears to be "taking the earth," especially in places where it is not wanted. It is widely distributed by birds that seem to thrive on the black fruit. The twining, woody vine climbs up, over, or under everything in its path, crowding out many

less aggressive plants. Its evergreen leaves are opposite, 3–4 inches long. The tubular flowers, borne in pairs in the leaf axils, are white, turning yellow on the second or third day. They have 5 conspicuous stamens. The flowers have a very pleasing fragrance. This plant was introduced from Asia. *East to Central Texas in thickets and open woods, border of woods, and along roadsides. March–July. Perennial.*

White honeysuckle, *L. albiflora*, has similar fragrant flowers. Its bright red fruit is a favorite bird food, assuring its wide distribution. *Central and West Texas; does best in the mountains. April–May.*

Sambucus canadensis
Elderberry

Elderberry is a large shrub, 5–10 feet tall, that grows in damp places, commonly along streams, ditches, or roadsides. It blooms mostly in late spring but occasionally in late summer. It often forms thickets.

The stem of the flower head has 5–7 branches (usually 5), each of which again branches 3 or 4 times before reaching the 5 fine branches that support the multiple, tiny flowers.

Leaves are composed of 5–11 leaflets with tiny pointed teeth. The opposite leaves are 4–12 inches long and a third as wide.

Flowers are fragrant and are arranged in large convex or flattened heads 4–10 inches across. Each creamy-white flower (green at first), is about ¼ inch across, trumpet-shaped, ending in 5 petal-like lobes. The fruit is a purplish-black berry ⅕ inch in diameter that is used widely for making wine and jelly. Birds eat the berries, which accounts for the plant's wide distribution.

The stems of this shrub have a large white pith in the center. Children often remove a section 6–10 inches long, hollow it out, and make a whistle from it; or, with a longer piece, make a blow-gun with which they can shoot cylindrical "bullets" a considerable distance. Photographed near Tyler in July. *East and Central Texas in rich, moist soil; rare in Panhandle. Late spring or summer. Perennial.*

————————————————

A similar species, commonly called blueberry elder (*S. caerulea*), is found in the Big Bend area. It has 5–7 leaflets to a leaf, narrowly oblong and finely toothed along the margins. Flower heads are similar, somewhat smaller, with blue berries that are also good for making wine and jellies.

CARYOPHYLLACEAE
Pink Family

The Pink Family can be distinguished by stems swollen at the nodes, leaves opposite (or whorled), usually without petioles, with margins entire. Flowers usually have 4 to 5 petals (absent, rarely) and 4 or 5 sepals, sometimes resembling petals, and either separate or united into a tube. The family includes the cultivated carnation as well as many beautiful wildflowers.

Silene laciniata
Catchfly

This eye-catching catchfly is found in the same general habitat preferred by the giant coral root orchid (*Hexelectris grandiflora*) under oak or madrone trees in the mountains from 5,000 to 6,000 feet. We found it there in the Davis Mountains on the upper reaches of Limpia Creek, where this one was photographed in September. It grows 10–15 inches tall and is unbranched. Leaves are alternate and slightly wavy, 1½–2½ inches long, and narrow. The flower stems are about 2 inches long, growing from the leaf axils, with 1–3 flowers on each. The sepals are united, forming a tube 1 inch long that encloses the flower which opens out flat into 5 petal-like lobes. Each lobe is deeply cut into 4 narrow sections, giving the flower a fringed effect. A whitish ring at the center surrounds the stamens and pistil. The stamens have green anthers.

Catchfly is so called because it generally has sticky bands around the stem between the upper leaves, in which small insects are often caught; however, this is not an insectivorous plant; it does not digest the insects. *Mountains of West Texas, 5,000–6,000 feet. May–October.*

Silene subciliata
Prairie-Fire Pink (Catchfly)

Prairie-fire pink is rare in Texas and we
have found only two plants, both in the
Big Thicket. We found the one shown here
while on a canoe trip down Village Creek,
near Parker's Pond, in October. It is an
erect plant, growing 1–3 feet tall, with opposite leaves, rather fleshy, up to 6 inches
long and ½ inch wide. The attractive
flowers are bright red with 5 petals, ½–¾
inch long, slightly toothed at the tip, and
folding backward slightly with the stamens protruding noticeably. *Big Thicket.
July–October. Perennial.*

Stellaria nuttallii
Chickweed

Chickweed grows 8–12 inches high and
is found in moist, low ground in prairies
and open woods. Leaves are opposite, and
the stems are enlarged at the joints. The
flowers are white, about 1 inch across, and
have 5 deeply notched broad petals. The
center of the flower is greenish, with
greenish streakings on the petals. The anthers are yellow. This one was photographed near Brenham in April. *Northeast
to Southwest Texas. April–May. Annual.*

COMMELINACEAE
Dayflower or Spiderwort Family

Members of the Dayflower Family have
jointed stems. The leaves are thick, succulent, grasslike in shape, sheathing at the
base. Flowers have 3 sepals, 3 petals, and
3–6 stamens. They grow in clusters, often
only one opening at a time. They wither
within a day or less, others taking their
place over a long blooming season. If they
are picked, the petals quickly become
pulpy or liquid; hence, they are sometimes known as Job's tears or widow's
tears.

Commelina communis
Dayflower

Close observation will remove the diffi-
culty in distinguishing between the genus
Commelina (dayflower) and the genus
Tradescantia (spiderwort), both of which
are in the family of Commelinaceae.
Flowers of the genus *Commelina* have 2
large petals and 1 small; those of *Tradescantia* have 3 petals equal in size. In this
species the upper 2 petals are blue and the
lower one is whitish, and smaller. The petals are attached by a thin strand called a
claw. Stamens are unequal: 3 long (one
of these curved inward), and 3 slightly
shorter. Photographed near Huntsville in
July. *East Texas. May–October.*

Commelina erecta
Dayflower

A number of species of *commelina* grow
throughout the state, blooming from May
to October. It is difficult to distinguish the
species. In most of them, the lower petal is
white, very small, and apt to be over-
looked. The buds are enclosed in 2 flat
bracts and do not show until the blossom
protrudes from within. This photo was
taken in the Davis Mountains in September. *West Texas. August–September.
Perennial.*

Tradescantia spp.
Spiderwort

Spiderwort plants are usually erect. The
leaves are alternate, often long and narrow.
The flowers grow in umbel-like clusters
with 1–3 leaflike bracts just beneath.
There are 3 sepals and 3 light-blue to rose-
violet or occasionally pure pink or white
petals, and 6 stamens. They often grow in
clumps in sunny spots in open woods and
prairies, and respond well to cultivation. It
is difficult to distinguish between the
species, the more so because they often
hybridize. This one was photographed at
McKinney Falls State Park, near Austin, in
June. *Statewide. March–June. Perennial.*

COMPOSITAE (ASTERACEAE)
Sunflower, Aster, or Daisy Family

The Sunflower Family is found all over the world and represents more than 20 percent of the wildflowers in Texas. They bloom from early spring to late autumn.

The outer circle of parts of most flowers in this family is made up of what an inexperienced person would call petals. Actually, each of these "petals" is a perfect flower with a strap-shaped petal, stamens, and a pistil; these are called ray flowers. The inner circle of parts is also made up of perfect flowers. These are tubular in shape, with stamens and pistil, and are called disc flowers. In most Compositae, including daisies, asters, and sunflowers, both types of flowers are present. However, some, such as the dandelion, have only ray flowers, while others, such as the thistles, have only disc flowers. In any case, every flower head is actually composed of several flowers; hence, the family name, Compositae (composites).

Flower heads vary greatly in size and appearance. Some are large and single, as in the sunflower; others are small and clustered, as in the yarrow. The head is usually surrounded by a whorl of bracts (or phyllaries), just below or embracing the flowering part.

Achillea millefolium
Yarrow

Yarrow grows to 3 feet tall and has no branches except near the top. The compound leaves are alternate, 3–5 inches long, with many leaflets on each side of the midrib; and these are further divided into smaller leaflets, giving them a delicate, fernlike, lacy appearance. Flower heads are arranged in large, compact clusters at the top of the stem, each cluster consisting of 1 or more flower heads. The flower head has 20–25 yellowish-white (rarely pink) ray flowers and similarly colored disc flowers. This is a good garden plant, as it can be used in fresh or dried arrangements and has a pleasing fragrance. Photographed near Kingsland in April. *North, East, and Central Texas; rarely, in the Davis Mountains. March–July. Perennial.*

Aster sagittifolius
Broad-leaved Aster

There are more than 650 species of the genus *Aster*, growing in all parts of the world except Australia. Some are low-growing, with 1 head to a stem; others are 4 feet tall with clusters of flower heads on many branches. There are various sizes and shapes of leaves. The flowers are light to dark purple, blue, or white, with 10–25 slender ray flowers and always a yellow center. There is much disagreement regarding species identification in *Aster*.

The broad-leaved aster grows to 4 feet tall with many branches. Leaves are simple, alternate. There are 10–15 ray flowers, light blue to purple or sometimes white, ⅛–½ inch long, with a yellow center. This one was photographed at Lake Tyler in October. *From Northeast Texas to the Gulf. September–November.*

Amblyolepis setigera
Huisache Daisy (Butterfly Daisy)

Huisache daisy is so called because it often grows in thick stands under the huisache and other chaparral bushes, forming an almost solid blanket of gold. It grows 6–15 inches tall, with several rough, hairy branches in the upper part. Leaves are without petioles, the upper ones having lobes at the base that extend almost around the stem. The large, yellow flower heads, 1¼–2 inches across, are on long stems that are bare on the upper portion. The yellow to orange-yellow center is dome-shaped, and the disc flowers are velvety. The 8–12 ray flowers are up to 1 inch long with 3 or 4 teeth on the rim. Often the toothed portion is noticeably lighter than the rest. The plant has a strong scent. Photographed between Kerrville and Junction in April. *South and Central Texas. March–June. Annual.*

————————————————

The late purple aster, *A. patens*, is also late blooming. It grows 1–3 feet tall and is easily recognized by its short, broad, rough leaves which are attached directly to the stems. Leaves are alternate. Flowers vary from violet to pink. *Dry woodlands throughout East and Central Texas. August–October.*

Baileya multiradiata
Desert Marigold (Paper Daisy, Desert Baileya)

An attractive flower that will compare favorably with any of its cultivated relatives, the desert marigold is found in Southwest Texas from the Davis Mountains to the Big Bend area, where it grows in profusion. We have seen it blooming continuously from Shafter to Boquillas Canyon—100 miles or more. Appealing in itself, its appearance was enhanced by being mixed with bluebonnets practically all the way, making both of them more attractive than either would be by itself. The plant is toxic to sheep and for that reason is not favored by ranchers.

The desert marigold grows to 18 inches tall; the bottom half is leafy. Leaves are deeply cut. Flower stems are 4–8 inches long. The flower head is deep yellow, about 1½ inches across, and it has 25–50 lightly toothed ray flowers. Photographed in the Big Bend in August. *Southwest Texas. March–November (intermittently).*

Berlandiera lyrata
Green-eyed Lyre Leaf

Green-eyed lyre leaf grows to 4 feet tall
and has a basal rosette of leaves, with others on the stem, some deeply cut into
rounded lobes. Each flower head has 8
yellow ray flowers with purplish veins beneath, slightly pinched in at the tip. The
disc flowers are maroon. When the ray
flowers drop, the green, flat bracts beneath
the blossom are more apparent. It is at this
point that the flowers appear "green-eyed"
and are very pretty in dried flower arrangements. We photographed this one in the
Davis Mountains in September. *Central
and West Texas. June–October. Perennial.*

Carduus nutans
Nodding Thistle (Musk Thistle)

Nodding thistles grow 2½–3 feet tall. The
heads droop slightly at the tip of the
stems, suggesting the common name.
The flower head is surrounded by several
rows of very sharp, green bracts in the
early stages, with only a small portion of
purple showing in the center of the green
as it begins to open. As it matures, the
rose-purple disc flowers protrude. There
are no ray flowers. The heads are up to
2 inches across. Often the three stages
of development will be seen on one
plant, as in the photo. Everything about
this plant is thorny. Photographed south of
Fredericksburg, in April. *Central Texas.
Biennial.*

Centaurea americana
Basket Flower (Star Thistle, Shaving Brush)

Centaurea cyanus
Cornflower (Bachelor's Button, Star Thistle)

All the flowers of the basket flower plant are tubular (though one would never know it without a hand lens) and divided into 5 long, narrow lobes, all looking like stamens except under close observation. The fully opened head has an outer border of many lavender flowers, with cream-colored flowers in the center. At maturity, the lavender flowers lie at right angles to those in the center, or droop downward. Before the flower is fully opened, however, it resembles an old-fashioned shaving brush. The name "basket flower" refers to the stiff, straw-colored bracts just beneath the flower head, which are divided at the tip into long, sharp teeth. Photographed in the Davis Mountains in July. *East-Central Texas west to the Trans-Pecos and northwest to the Panhandle. June– July; under favorable conditions, sometimes blooms again in August in the Trans-Pecos. Annual.*

C. cyanus was once a common flower in the wheatfields of England, where wheat was called "corn"; hence, the name "cornflower." In America it escaped cultivation and has spread widely. It grows 8–30 inches tall, with several branches near the top. The stem is thinly covered with whitish "wool." The bracts beneath the blossom have sharp, triangular teeth along their edges. The flower heads are ½–1 inch across and may be blue, white, pink, or purple. The ray flowers flare out into several fine divisions, giving the flower a feathery appearance. The disc flowers and ray flowers are generally the same color. Photographed near Tyler in June. *East, North-Central, and Northeast Texas. June–July. Annual.*

Chrysanthemum leucanthemum
Ox-eye Daisy

Chrysactinia mexicana
Damianita

A strongly scented, leafy shrub, damianita grows 1–2 feet tall, with many branches and thick, short, narrow leaves. The flower heads are golden yellow, 1 inch across, commonly with 8 narrow ray flowers, on slender stems at the end of the branches. This one was photographed in the Big Bend area in June. *Central and West Texas. June–October. Perennial.*

The ox-eye daisy is rare in Texas and is found only in the northeast corner. It grows 1–3 feet tall and tends to form colonies in fields or on roadsides. The lower leaves are oval and broader at the tip. Upper leaves are narrower, and often attached directly to the stem. All are unevenly lobed or toothed. The 20–30 ray flowers are white and nearly 1 inch long. The large center is yellow. This one was photographed near Paris in May. *Northeast Texas. May–October. Perennial.*

The blossom of *Aphanostephus skirrhobasis*, or lazy daisy, is like a smaller version of the ox-eye daisy. It grows to 2 feet high, and the flower heads are 1–2 inches across, 1 flower to a stem. The 20–45 ray flowers are ½ inch long, narrow, white to pink, and often deep red on the underside. The center is yellow. Leaves are alternate, ½–2½ inches long, the lower ones sharply toothed, the upper ones smooth. Stems and leaves have soft hairs. *Gulf Coast to lower Panhandle. March–July. Annual.*

Cirsium texanum
Texas Thistle

The Texas thistle grows 2–5 feet tall, without branches, or sparingly branched near the top. The numerous leaves are alternate, 4–9 inches long, smaller on the upper third of the stem. Leaves are green above and white below, with a woolly texture on the underside. The irregular lobes have spines at the tip but few elsewhere on the leaf. There is 1 flower head to a stem, with no ray flowers but numerous disc flowers which are deep rose-lavender. It grows throughout the state except in the Panhandle, from April to August. Bumblebees work the flowers when they mature. Photographed northwest of Bastrop in April. *Statewide except in the Panhandle. April–August. Biennial or perennial.*

————————————————

The bull thistle, *C. horridulum*, is similar to *C. texanum* in most respects. It grows 1–5½ feet tall, and the leaves are 8–24 inches long. In rare instances the blossom is yellow. *Primarily in the eastern third of the state. March–May. Winter annual or biennial.*

Coreopsis tinctoria
Coreopsis

Coreopsis is an erect to sprawling plant 1–4 feet high. Leaves are opposite, about 4 inches long, once or twice divided into long, narrow segments. The upper leaves are often undivided. There are numerous flower heads, 1¼ inches across, usually with 8 yellow ray flowers that have 4, sometimes 3, prominent lobes, brownish-red at the base. Disc flowers are also brownish-red, and the whole center of the flower often looks like beadwork. Photographed southwest of Paris in May. *Abundant over the eastern half of the state. May–August. Annual.*

—————————————

Tickseed, *C. lanceolata*, also found in the eastern half of the state, often lines the highways. It grows in small clumps, but forms extensive colonies. It is 1–2½ feet tall and has leaves 3–4 inches long, opposite, sometimes alternate near the top where the leaves are fewer. Some of the leaves are deeply cut, almost forming 3 leaflets. Flower heads are yellow, 1–1½ inches across. The yellow center or disc flowers stand out distinctly from the ray flowers, which appear to be attached just below them. Ray flowers are 4-lobed. *Eastern half of state. March–July. Perennial.*

Dyssodia acerosa
Prickleleaf Dogweed

Cosmos parviflorus
Southwest Cosmos

Southwest cosmos grows 2–3 feet tall and is branched several times in the upper half, with a single flower head, about 1¼ inches across, at the end of each slender, bare stem. It has 8 pale orchid ray flowers, with a yellow center. It is an attractive flower, suitable for cultivation, and seeds are commercially available. Leaves are threadlike, divided 2 or 3 times. It is not abundant, as it is grazed by livestock. Photographed in Madera Canyon, in the Davis Mountains, in September. *Grows in gravelly soil up to 7,500 feet elevation in West Texas. August–October. Annual.*

The dogweeds are strong-scented plants. Just walking through them stirs up a lingering, unpleasant odor. Prickleleaf dogweed is a small plant, 4–8 inches tall, growing from a woody stem with several branches near the base. It has many slender, sharp-pointed leaves less than 1 inch long. The bright yellow flower heads, less than 1 inch across, are clustered at the ends of short stems. Photographed in the Davis Mountains in April. *Grows throughout the Trans-Pecos. March–November. Perennial.*

————————————————————

Common dogweed, *D. pentachaeta*, is small and erect, 4–10 inches tall. It has many branches with slender, needle-like leaves about ½ inch long, divided into narrow lobes tipped with a spine. The flower heads, ½ inch across, are above the leaves at the end of stems about 3 inches long. They are yellow and numerous, with prominent protruding yellow centers. *West Texas. April–November. Perennial.*

Echinacea sanguinea
Purple Coneflower

The graceful purple coneflower has an un-branched stem that grows to 3 feet tall. Leaves are alternate and usually near the base, 4–10 inches long and ¼ inch wide. Upper leaves have long hairs. There is 1 flower head to each stem, with 10–20 ray flowers, often conspicuously drooping, rose-pink to pale purple, as much as 2 inches long and ⅛–¼ inch wide. The center is cone-shaped, 1 inch in diameter, and ¼–¾ inch high, purplish-brown on the outside ring and greenish in the center. This photo was taken in the Big Thicket in May. *Southeast Texas. May–June. Perennial.*

Engelmannia pinnatifida
Cut-leaved Daisy (Engelmann's Daisy)

This common plant of the plains and prai-ries closely resembles the sunflower but has the daisy characteristic of closing the flower heads at night and opening them in bright sunlight. The rough, hairy plants grow 1–3 feet tall and are topped by broad clusters of showy yellow flower heads about 1½ inches across. The 8–10 ray flowers are ½ inch long and are indented at the tip. The erect to spreading stems form a rounded crown. Leaves are alter-nate and deeply cut, 3–6 inches long. The upper leaves often have coarse teeth. Pho-tographed at McKinney Falls State Park, near Austin, in April. *Central and West Texas. April–July. Perennial.*

Erigeron philadelphicus
Fleabane Daisy

The fleabane daisy grows along roadsides
and in fields and woodlands. It has over
150 threadlike, white ray flowers. The center, disc flowers are 5-toothed and yellow,
and there are many flower heads to each
much-branched stem. The yellow center
with the large number of very fine ray
flowers is the best identification. They are
much finer than those of other daisies or
asters. Flower heads are ½–¾ inch across.
This one was photographed north of Tyler
in March. *Statewide; abundant in East
Texas. March–August. Perennial.*

——————————————————

Another species, *E. tenuis,* is very similar except that the leaves are narrower.
These two species are often found growing
together in East Texas, though *E. philadelphicus* is more abundant in the cal-
careous clay of North-Central Texas and
E. tenuis is more common in the sandy
soils of East Texas.

Eupatorium coelestinum
**Mistflower (Blue Boneset, Wild
Ageratum)**

Mistflower grows to 3 feet high, but often
lower, with leaves opposite, somewhat triangular in shape, and bluntly toothed. At
the top of the plant the branches, with
their short-stemmed clusters of flowers,
form an almost flat top. Disc flowers are
bright blue or violet, about ¼ inch long.
There are no ray flowers. This plant was
photographed on the lower Neches River
in May. *East and Southeast Texas; prefers
moist places. April–frost. Perennial.*

——————————————————

Several other species are found in Texas,
all with similar flowers but differing in
leaf structure. Some are adapted to dry
conditions. *E. wrightii* grows throughout
the Trans-Pecos and is abundant in the
Chisos, Davis, and Guadalupe mountains,
August–November. *E. greggii* also grows
in the Trans-Pecos, May–October.

Gaillardia aestivalis
Winkler Gaillardia

Winkler gaillardia grows 1–2 feet tall. The flower heads have 6–10 white ray flowers and a yellow center. The ray flowers are tubular at the base but flare out at the top into 3 deeply cut lobes. Leaves are 2–4 inches long, alternate, thick, with soft hair on both sides. Lower leaves are larger than those higher on the stem. Photographed near Parker's Pond, in the Big Thicket, in April. *East Texas. April– October. Perennial.*

————————————————————

The flower of *G. pinnatifida*, abundant in Central Texas, is much like the one shown here, except that the ray flowers are yellow, sometimes streaked red near the base, and the center is deep red. Ray flowers are 3-lobed but not so deeply cut as those of *G. aestivalis*.

Gaillardia multiceps
Gyp Indian Blanket

This West Texas perennial, usually 12–18 inches tall, has bare flower stems, with the leaves at the base of the plant. It is woody at the base. The ray flowers are yellow and deeply 3-lobed. When they fall, the brownish-red center remains, giving the plant a striking appearance. It blooms June to September as a rule, though we photographed this one in late April, west of Sanderson. *West Texas. June–September. Perennial.*

Gaillardia pulchella
Indian Blanket

The Indian blanket is a beautiful and impressive flower that grows along roadsides and in fields and pastures, sometimes covering large areas. We have seen 40 acres of these colorful flowers in almost a pure stand. It is also a good garden flower.

Flower heads are 1½–2 inches across, 1 on each main stem, which may be 4–8 inches long. Each has 10–20 ray flowers, sometimes all red, but usually marked with brilliant yellow on the ends of the rays, forming a yellow band along the outside. The disc flowers are brownish-red, but slightly yellow in the middle. The plant is widely branched at the base. Upper leaves are alternate, 2–2½ inches long, and smooth, but the lower ones have a few teeth. The plant grows 1–2½ feet tall. Photographed near Blanco State Park in April. *Statewide except in forests and in driest areas. April–June. Annual.*

Gymnosperma glutinosum
Gumhead

This plant grows 1½–2½ feet tall and branches from the base. The lower part of the stem is woody. Leaves are narrow and sticky, 1½–2½ inches long, mixed with clumps of smaller leaves that are both alternate and opposite on the same stem. Flower stems are branched at the end of the main stems, with the yellow flower heads in clusters. Individual heads have 1 or 2 yellow ray flowers about ¹⁄₁₆ inch long, 1–3 disc flowers, and 5–8 bracts. Photographed in the Davis Mountains in September. *Trans-Pecos. March–October.*

Helenium badium
Basin Sneezeweed

We photographed this attractive flower near the Chihuahuan Desert Research Institute, between Alpine and Fort Davis, in August. It is erect, 1–2½ feet tall, and very hairy except on the flower stems. The threadlike leaves are 1½–2 inches long and are concentrated below the naked flower stems, which are 4–8 inches long. Flowers bloom at the end of the stem and are 1–2 inches across. Ray flowers are yellow and 3-toothed at the end, generally pointing downward. The disc flowers are reddish-brown and almost spherical, with the ray flowers attached to the lower side of the sphere. *Statewide. July–October. Annual or perennial.*

Haplopappus ciliatus
Clasping-leaved Haplopappus

This rank-growing, bushy plant, up to 5 feet tall, has alternate leaves 1–1¾ inches long and half as wide, spiny-toothed, and clasping the stem half way around or more. It has a strong odor, neither pleasing nor disagreeable. The many rows of tough, green bracts that surround the flower head are quite attractive when it is in bud. The flower head is yellow, with 20–30 narrow, pointed ray flowers and many yellow disc flowers. Photographed near Alpine in August. *West Texas. August–September.*

Helenium drummondii
Fringed Sneezeweed

These beautiful flowers graced the edge of
a swampy area near Sour Lake in April.
They grow on slender, unbranched stems,
about 2–3 feet tall. Leaves are alternate,
thin and long, becoming mere bracts on
the upper half of the plant. There is 1
flower head at the end of each stem, with
10–16 yellow ray flowers, ¾–1 inch long
and toothed on the end. The center or disc
flowers are yellow and almost spherical.
The large blossoms at the end of long,
leafless stems attract the attention they
deserve. They often grow in patches in
damp, open areas. *Southeast Texas.
March–May. Perennial.*

Helianthus annuus
Common Sunflower

The tall, stout-stemmed, widely branched common sunflower grows to 10 feet tall, with a main stem 1½ inches in diameter. Stems are bristly. Leaves are alternate, coarsely toothed, 3–6 inches long, broad at the base and tapering to a fine point. The petiole is often as long as the leaf. Flower heads are 3½–5½ inches across, growing singly at the top of the flower stem. The ray flowers are 1–2 inches long, often overlapping. The disc flowers are dark brown and about 1½ inches across. We have counted over 30 flower heads on 1 plant. Photographed near Bryan in July. *Grows throughout most of Texas. June–November. Annual.*

—————————————————

H. hirsutus, only 12–18 inches tall, also grows over most of Texas, but is especially abundant in East Texas, June–November. Leaves are finely toothed, up to 6 inches long, tapering from 2 inches wide at the base to a fine point at the end. Stems and leaves are bristly. Ray flowers are 1 inch long and yellow. Disc flowers are brownish to yellow.

Ashy helianthus, *H. mollis*, is an erect plant which grows 2–6 feet tall, branched in the upper part. The leaves and stems are covered with rough hairs. Leaves are opposite, 2–5 inches long, half as wide, and sharply toothed. Flower heads are 3–5 inches across, with 15–25 yellow ray flowers, deeply veined, about 2 inches long. The numerous disc flowers are also yellow. *East Texas. April–October. Perennial.*

Helianthus maximiliani
Maximilian Sunflower

An unusual perennial, Maximilian sunflower grows 2–10 feet tall. The leaves are
long and narrow, up to 10 inches near the
bottom and as short as 2 inches near the
top. They are alternate, coarse and hairy,
slightly wavy on the edges, often folded
lengthwise, slightly toothed and very
pointed. The yellow flowers, scattered
along the upper half of the plant, grow
from the leaf axils on stems 12 inches long
at the bottom to 3 inches near the top.
The flower head is up to 5 inches across,
with 15–19 ray flowers, deeply veined and
slightly toothed on the tip. The center is 1
inch or more across, green to dark brown.
Photographed near Kerrville in September.
Central Texas; prefers rich, loamy soil.
June–October. Perennial.

Hymenopappus artemisiaefolius
Old Plainsman (Woolly-White)

This flower is common over all East Texas
and is seen along roadsides and uncultivated land, where it often covers large
areas. It is erect, 2–4 feet tall, and
branched only in the upper part. Flower
heads are at the end of stems, sometimes
having as many as 60 florets in a cluster.
The bracts supporting the flower are
snowy white on the outer half, giving the
whole head a white appearance. Disc
flowers are rose-colored to dark wine, and
there are no ray flowers. The flowers are
funnel-shaped, 5-lobed (as all disc flowers
are), and numerous. This one was photographed at Caddo Lake in April. *East*
Texas. April–June. Biennial.

Liatris elegans
Gay Feather (Blazing Star)

Gay feather is a slender, unbranched plant, 1–4 feet tall. Its narrow leaves, much like pine needles, are about 3 inches long, whorled around the stem. The flower spike is 6–20 inches long, blooming from the top downward. Flowers are purple to pale lavender-pink, about ½ inch long. There are no ray flowers, but long, petal-like bracts the same color as the disc flowers are often mistaken for them. Photographed 5 miles east of Kountze in August. *Big Thicket. August–October. Perennial.*

————————————————

Other species are found widely over Texas to the Big Bend and the Davis Mountains. Species identification is difficult because the species have a tendency to cross. *L. squarrosa* has a spike of flowers like *L. elegans*, but the flowers are separate on the stem, not touching. It is found in East Texas in September and October.

False liatris, *Carphephorous pseudo-liatris*, is a similar plant, 2 feet tall, the flowers confined to the top of the stem. It grows in Southeast Texas.

Lindheimera texana
Texas Star

Texas star plants are 6–24 inches tall and widely branched. Stems and branches are hairy. The lower leaves are alternate and coarsely toothed, but the upper ones are opposite and smooth on the edges, 2–2½ inches long. There are 1 to several flower heads in a cluster at the end of each stem. Each flower head has 5 bright yellow ray flowers, each with 2 prominent veins and indented at the tip. Flower heads are 1–1¼ inches across. Photographed near Bonham in May. *Woods and prairies of Northeast and Central Texas. March–May. Annual.*

Lygodesmia texana
**Texas Skeleton Weed (Purple
Dandelion, Flowering Straw)**

Texas skeleton weed grows 12–15 inches
tall, with smooth, almost leafless stems.
Its few leaves are at the base of the plant
and are narrow, gray-green, with short
lobes. The bare stems, growing at odd
angles, suggest its common name. The
flower heads, rose to lavender and 2 inches
across, grow singly at the end of flower
stems. Only 1 flower head blooms at a
time on each slender, forking stem. The
bracts form a tube about 1 inch long, and
the flower head extending from it opens
out almost flat. It has 12 ray flowers and
orchid-colored disc flowers that curl toward the center. Each ray has 5 minute
teeth at the tip. When the stems are broken, they exude sap which coagulates into
a gum. This specimen was photographed
in the Davis Mountains in August. *On
prairies throughout most of the state.
May–September. Perennial.*

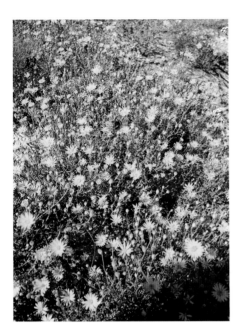

Machaeranthera wrightii
Gyp Daisy

Most species of *Machaeranthera* have at some time been placed in the *Aster* genus, so if the Gyp daisy looks like an *Aster* to you, you are in good company. The stems, woody near the base, are covered with sticky hairs. Leaves are widest near the tip and sometimes have spiny teeth. The flower heads, usually slightly cupped, are on long stems and have 20–30 lavender ray flowers about ¾ inch long. Disc flowers are yellow. This photograph was taken near Terlingua in May. *West Texas. May–October. Annual.*

Machaeranthera gracilis
Slender Goldenweed

This little flower makes up in numbers what it lacks in size. Sometimes it covers large areas, 1 or 2 acres, with its bright yellow flowers. It grows 10–15 inches tall, with many narrow leaves, ⅛–¼ inch long, the lower ones shallowly toothed. The stiff branches, 1–3 inches long, are on the upper half of the main stem, with 1 flower head at the end of each. Each flower head, ½–¾ inch across, has 20–30 ray flowers and many disc flowers. Photographed in the Davis Mountains in September. *West Texas. August–November. Annual.*

The tansy aster, *M. tanacetifolia*, usually has many branches, is bushy, and grows 8–15 inches high. Leaves are alternate, the upper ones pinnately compound, the lower ones twice divided. Bracts are green and feathery. Flower heads are at the end of the branches and are 1¼–2 inches across with 15–25 lavender ray flowers. The disc flowers are yellow. The tansy aster is used in gardens. *In the wild, restricted to Panhandle and Trans-Pecos. May–October. Annual.*

Melampodium leucanthum
Arnica (Plains Blackfoot)

The flower heads of this plant grow in a dense, rounded pattern that at first glance resembles a large bouquet. Plants are seldom over 6 inches high, and the clump is 1–2 feet across. Each flower head is 1 inch across or less and has 8–11 ray flowers, with 2 or 3 broad teeth at the tip. They bloom at the tip of a short branch that grows from the axils of the upper leaves. The yellow-orange disc flowers contrast sharply with the white ray flowers. Photographed east of Presidio in March. *Trans-Pecos; abundant from Davis Mountains to Big Bend. March–October. Perennial.*

Palafoxia hookeriana
Sand Palafox

We photographed the sand palafox on the banks of Village Creek on the east side of the Big Thicket, in October. It grows 16–40 inches tall and is unbranched except for the numerous flower stems on the upper third. It is lightly covered with hair, and somewhat sticky. Leaves are 4 inches long or less and ¾ inch wide. Flower heads have 8–12 rose-colored ray flowers, deeply 3-toothed and about ½ inch long, and many rose-colored disc flowers. The flower is quite attractive and is often used in yard plantings. *Grows in sandy soil in Southeast Texas. September–October. Annual.*

Pectis angustifolia
Crownseed Pectis

Perezia wrightii
Pink Perezia

This aromatic herb grows to 10 inches tall. A crushed leaf has a lemon-scented aroma and is good in tea. The leaves are grasslike, with a strong vein down the center, 3–5 inches long. The heads are bunched at the ends of the branches. The flower heads, about 2 inches across, have 8–10 short rays. This one was photographed in Big Bend National Park in September. *Mountains of West Texas. August–October.*

Pink perezia grows 1½–2 feet tall and has many branches. The leaves, 1–5 inches long, are simple, alternate, with a short petiole or none at all. They are slightly wavy on the edges and finely toothed. The fragrant, rose-pink flower heads are massed in clusters at the top of the stems. They are ¾ inch across, made up of 8–12 florets. This one was photographed on the Scenic Loop in the Davis Mountains in September. *Trans-Pecos. March–November.*

Pericome caudata
Tail-leaf Pericome

Tail-leaf pericome grows to 5 feet tall and is often 5 feet across at the top. It is woody at the base, very leafy, and tends to sprawl. The upper leaves, about 1 inch long on short petioles, are alternate, triangular, tapering to a long tip; the lower leaves are much longer and opposite. Each branch has 1–5 yellow flower heads, 1–1½ inches across, on stems less than 1 inch long that grow from the leaf axils on the main stem. They have many disc flowers but no ray flowers. They grow in the mountains of West Texas. The ones we have seen were at elevations of 4,000 feet or more. We photographed this one in Green Gulch, in the Chisos Mountains, in September. *Mountains of West Texas. August–November. Perennial.*

Pinaropappus roseus
Rock Lettuce (White Dandelion, Pink Dandelion)

Rock lettuce grows to 6 inches tall. Flower heads are white with a yellow center, 2 inches across, with ray flowers of varied lengths, noticeably squared off at the ends, with fine teeth. They close by mid-morning. Both the stems and the leaves contain a milky sap. Leaves are mostly at ground level, narrow and often lobed halfway to the midrib. It is said that the undersides of the petals are pink to rose-lavender and that the upper side is sometimes pale pink, which would agree with the "pink dandelion" name. In those we have seen, however, we have not found this to be true. Photographed near Comstock in April. *South-Central Texas to the Davis Mountains. March–August. Perennial.*

Pluchea purpurascens
Southern Marsh Fleabane

Southern marsh fleabane grows to 2 feet
tall or more, in marshes or other areas
that are always moist. It has several leafy
branches on the upper part, none below.
Leaves vary, some long and narrow, and
some broad at the base, 2–4 inches long,
pointed at the tip, and irregularly toothed
on the margins. The fragrant, rose-colored
flowers grow in small heads in a flat-
topped cluster at the end of the stems.
Photographed near Saratoga in September.
*Found in salt marshes throughout the
state. July–September. Annual.*

Psilostrophe tagetina
Woolly Paperflower

This plant is typical of many in the dry
Southwest in having a dense covering of
woolly white hairs which enable it to
withstand arid conditions by reducing
the loss of moisture. The flower heads,
1–1½ inches across, have 3–5 ray flowers
much broader than long and conspicuously 3-lobed. Both ray and disc flowers
are bright yellow. The flower heads are
densely clustered on short branches at the
top of stems 6–24 inches long. They remain on the stem unusually long, even
after the seeds are formed, eventually becoming papery. Leaves are alternate, about
1 inch long and ¼ inch wide. Plants grow
in clumps. Photographed west of Sanderson in April. *Trans-Pecos. February–
October.*

Pyrrhopappus carolinianus
Texas Dandelion (False Dandelion)

The Texas dandelion is common throughout the eastern half of the state. It grows
in pastures and along roadsides, but seems
to do best on lawns. It often has several
erect stems, 6–20 inches long, which exude a milky substance when broken.
Large, deeply lobed leaves, 2–6 inches
long, grow from the base of the plant on
petioles half as long as the leaves themselves. The few upper leaves are alternate,
much smaller, with little indentation. The
flower heads are 1–1½ inches across, 1
flower head to a stem. Both ray and disc
flowers are yellow. This was photographed
at McKinney Falls State Park near Austin
in April. *Eastern half of state. March–
May. Annual.*

Ratibida columnaris
Long-headed Coneflower (Mexican Hat, Thimbleflower)

We have photographed the eye-catching long-headed coneflower in many parts of the state but these photographs were taken 5 miles east of Canton. In East Texas these flowers are often 3½ feet tall. Leaves are alternate, 2–4½ inches long, deeply cut into 5–9 narrow segments. Both leaves and stems are somewhat rough, with the upper third of the stem bare. There is 1 flower head to a stem, with ray flowers ¾–1 inch long, yellow-orange, often with deep reddish-orange at the base, and velvety. Sometimes they are entirely yellow, and in other cases only the tips are yellow. Often the rays bend downward. The center is erect, conelike, 1–2 inches long, gray-green, turning brown as it matures. *Fields, roadsides, and open woods from East Texas through the Trans-Pecos and to the Panhandle. May–July, or later, depending on rains. Perennial.*

Rudbeckia grandiflora
Tall Coneflower

The erect, coarse tall coneflower grows
2½–5 feet tall and usually forms colonies.
The stem and leaves have rough hairs.
Leaves at the bottom of the plant have
long petioles, but the higher ones attach
directly to the main stem. They are 2½–6
inches long and half as wide, shallow-
toothed with prominent ribs. Flower heads
have 8–12 ray flowers, ¾–1 inch long,
yellow and drooping. The cones are ¾–1¼
inches high, gray-green, but turning brown
as the flowers mature. Honey bees, bugs,
butterflies, and beetles feed on the nectar
and pollen. This coneflower is a desirable
ornamental and does well in cultivation.
Photographed near Tyler in July. *East
Texas, extending west to Corsicana,
Madisonville, and beyond. Perennial.*

Rudbeckia hirta
Black-eyed Susan (Brown-eyed Susan)

Black-eyed Susan is a rough, hairy plant,
1–2½ feet tall. Leaves are alternate, 1–4½
inches long, and lightly toothed. There are
many branches, each with a single flower
head at the end, 1½–2 inches in diameter.
Ray flowers are yellow, often drooping at
the ends. The center resembles that of a
coneflower, but it is dark brown and not
so high. Photographed near Lake Tyler in
June. *Widely distributed in prairies and
pinelands; especially abundant in East
and South Texas. May–September.
Perennial.*

Senecio ampullaceus
Texas Groundsel (Ragwort)

Senecio is one of the largest genera of
flowering plants, and many grow in Texas.
The species are difficult to identify, as
there are many different sizes and shapes
of leaves and other minute differences; but
all have narrow, yellow ray flowers,
rounded on the end, and yellow disc
flowers. Ray flowers are often turned
backward, exposing the disc flowers completely. Every part of the state has one or
more species of *Senecio.*

   S. ampullaceus grows 1–2 feet tall.
Leaves clasp the stem and are 1–3 inches
long, with 1 main vein down the center.
The yellow flower heads are on stems
growing out of the leaf axils near the top
of the plant, with 2–4 blossoms on each
stem, 1–1¼ inches across. There are 7–9
ray flowers per flower head. Photographed
at McKinney Falls State Park, near Austin,
in April. *Open places throughout East
and South-Central Texas. March–May.
Annual.*

——————————————————

Yellow-top butterweed, *S. glabellus,* is
an attractive plant, especially when it
blankets many acres with the sun shining
across the plants. It grows 1–3 feet tall
and has a rosette of leaves at the base from
which the main stem rises. It may be
single or branched. The alternate leaves
are lobed and toothed, ¾–2¾ inches long.
The flower head is 1 inch across, with
yellow ray and disc flowers. *East Texas;
prefers wet areas. March–May. Annual.*

   S. greggii grows 12–18 inches high, with
delicate, alternate leaves attached directly
to the stem. They are pinnately compound, each leaflet unevenly and roundly
lobed. The heads are ¾ inch across with
11–13 ray flowers each. The plant is
branched near the top, with all branches
forming a more or less flat top with many
flower heads on each short stem. *Common in East and South-Central Texas.
Spring–summer. Annual.*

Solidago altissima
Goldenrod

The monarch butterfly caught in this picture, along with dozens of others, was working a patch of goldenrod near Batson, on the west side of the Big Thicket, in November. The plant grows 2½–5 feet tall, with alternate, finely toothed leaves, 3–4 inches long, attached directly to the stem. The yellow flower heads, ¼ inch across, are crowded on 1 side of each of the many arching branches. *Often found on uncultivated land over the eastern third of the state; less frequently to the Trans-Pecos. July–November. Perennial.*

Numerous species of goldenrod occur in Texas. The innumerable tiny yellow flower heads in plumelike clusters are its most identifying feature. *S. sparsiflora* grows 2–3 feet tall. The middle and upper leaves are without petioles and smaller than the lower ones. They are sparingly toothed or smooth-edged. We found this species on Mt. Emory in the Chisos Mountains. *West Texas. July–October. Perennial.*

Tetraneuris linearifolia
Four-nerved Daisy

When one is walking across a bone-dry desert, where nothing is visible but sand and rocks, and comes across this delicate flower, 5 inches high, it commands attention. The few leaves are at the base, 2 inches long, forming a rosette. The stem is leafless and bears 1 yellow flower head that has 6–15 ray flowers. They are toothed, with 4 veins that converge at the tip. Photographed between San Vicente and the Chisos Mountains, in Big Bend National Park, in April. They grow larger under more favorable conditions. *Western two-thirds of the state. February–June. Annual.*

————————————————

Yellow daisy, *T. scaposa*, is usually less than 1 foot high. It has a cluster of stiff, rough leaves crowded around the base from which grow 1 or 2 leafless flower stems, 1 flower head on each. The flower head is about 1½ inches across, with 12 or more ray flowers, yellow with a slightly pinkish cast, each with 3 small teeth and 4 purple veins that converge at the tip. *Trans-Pecos. March–May; when rains are favorable, blooms again in August– September. Perennial.*

Thelesperma flavodiscum
Greenthread

T. flavodiscum is 28–36 inches tall, with 1–3 stems growing from the base, usually branching in the upper portion. The leaves are opposite,.mostly near the base of the stem, once or twice divided into thread-like segments, about 3 inches long. There are many yellow flower heads with 8 ray flowers about ⅝ inch long, each with 4 teeth at the tip. The disc flowers are also yellow. This plant was photographed in the Big Thicket in May. *Southeast Texas. June–August. Annual.*

————————————————

Another species, *T. simplicifolium*, grows to 20 inches tall and has many loosely branched stems. Leaves are opposite, 1–3 inches long. The lower leaves have 3–5 narrow segments, but those above have fewer. Flower heads are generally similar to those of *T. flavodiscum*, with 6–9 yellow ray flowers and yellowish-brown disc flowers. *West Texas. July–October.*

Verbesina encelioides
Golden Crownbeard (Butter Daisy)

This annual herb, 3–4 feet tall, grows over much of the Trans-Pecos. We have found it along the Rio Grande from El Paso to Del Rio. It also grows well in East Texas. The rough leaves are greenish-gray, 2–3 inches long and half as wide at the base, with large, sharp teeth. The flower heads are at the end of long, leafless stems. They are 1–1½ inches across, with orange disc flowers and yellowish-orange ray flowers. This one was photographed between Redford and Lajitas in September. *Very frequent in disturbed soils throughout most of Texas. June–September. Annual.*

——————————————————

Dwarf crownbeard, *V. nana*, gets its name from the fact that it rarely grows more than 6 inches tall. Its branches grow horizontally as a rule. Leaves are 2 inches long with sharp-toothed margins. The flower heads are 1½ inches across. The bright, lemon-yellow ray flowers are short in relation to the size of the flower head. Disc flowers are slightly brownish-yellow. *Trans-Pecos. May–October.*

Vernonia baldwinii
Ironweed

Ironweed grows 2–4 feet tall and has numerous leaves 3–4 inches long and ½ inch wide, attached directly to the stem. It branches considerably at the top, each stem with a rather flat head of purple flowers. It has only disc flowers. Buds are cream-colored before they open. This attractive plant is worthy of cultivation. One or more species of Ironweed, all with similar flowers, are found in all parts of the state blooming from June to November. This one was photographed in the Big Thicket in September. *Frequent in North-Central Texas, Edwards Plateau, and Plains country; infrequent in East Texas. June–September. Perennial.*

Viguiera cordifolia
Heartleaf Goldeneye

Heartleaf goldeneye is an erect perennial 3–4 feet tall with clusters of flower heads about 1 inch across at the ends of the branching stems. Each head has 10–12 bright yellow ray flowers, and yellow disc flowers. The leaves and stems are covered with coarse hair. Leaves are broadest at the base and sharply pointed. Photographed in the Davis Mountains in September. *Davis and Glass mountains in West Texas. August–November. Perennial.*

————————————————
Skeleton goldeneye, *V. stenoloba*, grows 2–4 feet tall. The leaves are divided into grasslike, narrow lobes. The flower heads are 1 inch across on slender stalks. The yellow ray flowers are deeply veined and the disc flowers are golden or brownish-yellow. *Big Bend area; Davis Mountains. June–October.*

A similar plant, yellow sleepy daisy, *Xanthisma texanum*, var. *drummondii* has lemon-yellow flowers that do not open until about noon; hence, the name "sleepy daisy." The flower head is 1½ inches across and grows at the tip of the stems. The plant grows 10–30 inches tall, with alternate leaves attached directly to the stem. The lower ones are larger, 1–2½ inches long, and deeply lobed or toothed. Upper leaves are rarely toothed. *Sandy woods and fields and along roadsides throughout Texas except in the northeast and the extreme west. May–October. Annual.*

Xanthocephalum dracunculoides
Common Broomweed

This broomweed, common in West Texas, is densely branched, with many slender stems and leaves, somewhat sticky throughout. It is 2–3 feet tall and 2–4 feet across and grows from 1 central root. The flower heads are numerous and small, ⅛–¼ inch across. It sometimes covers large areas, giving a pleasing yellow cast; however, it is not welcome on the range because it shades the ground, taking both sunshine and much-needed moisture from the grasses. It is an indicator of poor soil.

Broomweed is harvested by the truckload in West Texas for use in dried flower arrangements. In the past it was used extensively in making brooms, giving it the common name. It grows all over the Trans-Pecos. This one was photographed in the Davis Mountains in October. *West Texas. June–October. Perennial.*

Threadleaf broomweed, *X. microcephalum*, is a woody plant, 1–3 feet tall, with many branches, especially in the upper part. It is sometimes 3–4 feet across the top of the spreading branches, which give the plant a somewhat rounded appearance. The narrow leaves are ½–1½ inches long, alternate, with bunches of smaller, narrower leaves in their axils. There are many florets in each of the flower heads, which are located at the tips of the branches. They are yellow, ¼ inch across, with 5 ray flowers and 1–3 disc flowers. *Trans-Pecos. June–October. Perennial.*

Xanthocephalum gymnospermoides
Gummy Broomweed (Gummy Snakeweed)

Gummy broomweed grows 2–2½ feet tall, with several branches in the upper section. It has a sticky, gummy secretion on the bright golden flower heads, sometimes completely covering the large center, which is ⅜ inch across. The ray flowers are short, only ⅛ inch long. There are about 20 flower heads to a stem, and they are quite showy when growing in dense masses. The stems are often used to kindle fires because of the resin they contain. Photographed on the Scenic Loop in the Davis Mountains in September. *Trans-Pecos. August–October. Perennial.*

Zinnia grandiflora
Prairie Zinnia

The little prairie zinnia grows in low, rounded clumps about 8 inches high. The flower stems branch near the top with 1 or 2 flower heads to a stem. Flower heads are ¾–1¼ inches across. The 3–6 yellow ray flowers are almost round. As the blossom matures and the seeds form, the ray flowers cling to the base. With age, the ray flowers become papery and the disc flowers turn from yellow to reddish-brown.

It is easy for one not familiar with this flower to confuse it with the woolly paper-flower, *Psilostrophe tagetina*, as they both grow in clumps, both are yellow with a variable number of ray flowers, and both become papery as they mature. A distinction easy to recognize is that the ray flowers of the zinnia are not toothed while those of the paperflower are 3-toothed.

This zinnia was photographed in the Davis Mountains in July. *From Central Texas throughout the Trans-Pecos. May–October.*

————————————————

Dwarf zinnia, *Z. acerosa*, usually grows 4–10 inches tall with numerous branches and many narrow leaves, ¾–1½ inches long. The flower heads have 5–7 white to off-white ray flowers, and yellow disc flowers. The ray flowers are lightly toothed at the tip. The plant has a long blooming period. *From the Guadalupe Mountains to Del Rio. June–October.*

CONVOLVULACEAE
Morning-Glory Family

Texas members of the Morning-Glory Family consist mostly of twining or trailing plants, with a few erect, woody species. The petals, except in one genus, are joined to form the shape of a funnel or trumpet, often flaring at the end into a disc with 5 lobes, or none at all. The blossoms of most species are twisted or rolled up in bud, and often twist again as they wither. There are 5 stamens and a single compound pistil with 1–4 stigmas. The sweet potato and dodder, a parasite of other flowering plants, are members of this family.

Ipomoea sagittata
Salt-Marsh Morning Glory

Nothing can transform a humble cabin into a mansion quicker than a morning glory vine, and Texas is fortunate in having several species. The salt-marsh morning glory prefers the prairies along the coast, growing along the marshes and waterways. Its flowers are pink to reddish-purple, up to 3½ inches in diameter, on long stems that extend from the leaf axils. The vines twine over surrounding vegetation, usually forming colonies. Leaves are shaped like arrowheads, 1½–4 inches long. This was photographed near Houston in July. *Coastal prairies. April– October. Perennial.*

Another attractive species, the crestrib, *I. costellata*, prefers an opposite habitat, and is found in the Davis Mountains, a mile higher than *I. sagittata*. It remains more or less upright until it matures, then twines over surrounding vegetation. Leaves are palmate, with 5–9 segments. The flowers are pale lavender, ½ inch across, on the end of a long flower stem. *From Central Texas to the Trans-Pecos. July–October.*

Ipomoea trichocarpa
Wild Morning Glory

This funnel-shaped flower is orchid with a
deep purple center, 1–1½ inches across
and about the same length. The flower has
obvious lines that divide it into 5 sections,
and within each of these sections is a
lighter purple triangle, the 5 forming a star
within the flower. It has 2 kinds of leaves:
one divided into 3 sections, the other undivided; and the leaf stems are as long as
the leaves. This attractive morning glory
has trailing stems that grow to 15 feet long
or more. The one plant in the photo completely covered a bridge abutment. Photographed about 20 miles west of Del Rio
in October. *Abundant in Central Texas,
but also found farther west. May–
October. Perennial.*

Scarlet morning glory, *I. cristulata*, is the
only bright red morning glory in Texas
and is somewhat smaller than the others.
It grows on rocky slopes in the Davis
Mountains and is a twining vine with
deeply 3-lobed leaves. The flower tube is
¾–1½ inches long, opening out at the end
into an undivided blossom with prominent stamens. *Davis Mountains. July–
November. Perennial.*

Still another beautiful morning glory is
I. purpurea. Its blossoms may be blue, red,
white, purple, or mixed. Two or more
flowers often grow on the same flower
stem, originating at the leaf axils; they are
1½–3 inches long. Leaves are heart-shaped
with prominent veins. *Eastern half of
state. July–October. Perennial.*

CORNACEAE
Dogwood Family

Shrubs or small trees make up the Dogwood Family. Leaves are opposite with
short stems, simple, entire, or toothed,
with prominent pinnate veins. Flowers are
small, in umbels, cymes, or heads, often
with showy pink or white bracts. There
are 4 sepals, 4 petals, 4 stamens, and 1
pistil, which has an inferior ovary.

Cornus florida
Dogwood

This shrub or tree grows to 40 feet high
and is widespread in the woods of East
Texas. "Dogwood trails" attract many visi-
tors each spring. The beauty of the dogwood is not in the flowers, as one might
expect, but in the four broad, creamy-
white, petal-like bracts, 1¼–2½ inches
across, which surround the floral cluster.
The bracts are indented at the outer edge
because, before they open, they are attached at this point.

The minute, greenish-white flowers
have four petals and, with their accom-
panying bracts, bloom in March and April
before the leaves appear. The leaves are
3–5 inches long and 1½–2½ inches wide,
on ¾ inch stems. They are shiny green
above, paler below, heavily veined and
lightly toothed. The tree is beautiful
in the fall also, its leaves turning to all
shades of red, pink, and brown and bearing
scarlet fruit about ½ inch long. Some
states have laws against cutting dogwood.
It contains quinine in all parts, and scarlet
dye can be made from the bark. It is said
that the plant gets its name from the fact
that the bark of an English dogwood was
used to treat mangy dogs. Photographed
near Tyler. *East Texas. Flowers March–
April; fruits November. Perennial.*

CRUCIFERAE
Mustard Family

The flowers of the Mustard Family are white, purple, pink, or yellow. They have 4 petals which are opposite each other in pairs, forming a cross, which gives the family its Latin name, Cruciferae. The flowers are generally in a raceme. At flowering time the raceme may be short, with all the flowers on 1 level (flat-topped), the outermost flowers opening first. There are 4 sepals; usually 6 stamens, 2 lower than the others; 1 pistil, which becomes a 2-chambered pod in fruit. There are 2 types of fruit. One type is long and thin (silione), and one is short and wide (siliele). The leaves vary greatly. Juice from the stems is hot and biting.

This is a very large family of *primarily* spring-flowering plants. Correct identification of species requires detailed examination of the plant in many cases.

Lesquerella fendleri
Fendler Bladderpod (Popweed)

Fifteen species of bladderpods grow in Texas, and all have pea-sized bladderlike pods which pop when stepped on; hence the common name, popweed.

Fendler bladderpod is a silvery plant, 6–8 inches high, with mostly erect stems. All the leaves are narrow, some toothed, 1–2 inches long. The 4 petals are often ⅖ inch long and yellow. It is one of the most abundant perennial mustards and is found throughout the Big Bend area, where it is browsed by deer when other vegetation is scarce. Photographed in the Big Bend area in March. *West Texas. January–March. Perennial.*

Streptanthus platycarpus
Broadpod Twistflower

This plant has purple flowers, 1–1½
inches across, with flat-lying petals that
suggest the face of an old windmill. The
leaves are alternate, nearly round, and the
lower part clasps the stem. Photographed
near Van Horn in May. *Grows in limestone soils throughout the Trans-Pecos.
February–June. Annual.*
——————————————
Another mustard, abundant in the Davis
Mountains, is mountain or Hesper mustard, *Sisymbrium linearifolium*. It grows
tall and slender with a few blossoms at the
top. With favorable rains it may grow to 4
feet and bloom in September, beyond its
usual flowering time. The leaves are 2–3
inches long, and the lavender flowers are
½ inch across. *Widespread in West Texas,
especially in woodland mountains.
March–August. Annual.*

Thelypodium wrightii
Wright Thelypody

Wright thelypody is abundant on the
rocky slopes of the Davis Mountains,
where we photographed it in August.
Some plants were 6 feet tall. It has many
spreading branches with round clusters of
white flowers at the end of the stems. If
the flower heads were of different colors,
the plant would look like a decorated
Christmas tree. Long seedpods follow the
blossoms. These, with the long, narrow
leaves swaying in the breeze, give a delicate, lacy effect. *Mountains of West Texas.
July–October.*
——————————————
A white-blossomed mustard is pepper-
grass, *Lepidium montanum*, also known
as pennycress. It has the usual 4 petals of
the Mustard Family, and the flower clusters appear at the ends of the stems, with
many individual flowers which are ¼ inch
across. The pods are flat. *Central and
West Texas. March–June. Annual.*

CUCURBITACEAE
Gourd Family

The Gourd Family consists of vines with coiling tendrils and leaves borne singly. Flowers are either bell-shaped and lobed or have 5 spreading lobes on a long or short tube, and are yellow, greenish, or white. Each flower is either male or female. There are usually 3 stamens, sometimes 5, joined by their stalks or their tips. The ovary is inferior.

There are over 100 genera and 900 species in this large family, cultivated members of which include watermelon, cantaloupe, squash, pumpkin, and cucumber.

Cucurbita foetidissima
Buffalo Gourd (Stink Gourd)

We have photographed the buffalo gourd from May to September, but we have never seen it grow more prolifically than in the Davis Mountains in August 1981, when this photograph was made. The plants are often 20–30 feet across, with rough, hairy leaves as much as 12 inches long. The large, bell-like flowers, 2–4 inches long, are yellow to orange, 5-lobed at the opening, with stamens that have large anthers deep inside the throat. The globular fruits, about 4 inches across, are green-striped when young, maturing to tennis-ball size and turning yellow. The plant supposedly gets the name "stink gourd" from its foul odor, but we handled the fruit and dissected the blossoms without noticing any unpleasant odor. *Prairies, roadsides, and fields throughout Texas. May–September. Perennial.*

Ibervillea lindheimeri
Balsam Apple, Balsam Gourd

This gourd has tubular flowers with 5
spreading lobes, creamy-yellow, about ½
inch wide. Leaves are 1½–3¼ inches long
with 3–5 lobes, deeply cut and fine-
toothed. The fruit is over 1 inch in diameter, with green stripes when young, but
bright red when ripe. Before maturing it
has a spiny-looking green covering which
it sheds as it develops. The vine climbs
6–10 feet high by means of tendrils. Photographed in the Big Thicket, near Saratoga, in November. *In thickets and open
woods and on fences, eastern third of
state; rarely, in the Trans-Pecos. April–
November. Perennial.*

DROSERACEAE
Sundew Family

Members of the Sundew Family are found in acid bogs and capture insects with one of several methods. The sundew (*Drosera*) traps insects with sticky hairs on the leaves. The Venus' flytrap (*Dionaea*), which is not found in Texas, has leaf blades that fold up when an insect triggers them. All flower parts are in fives, regular, and perfect. The inflorescence is rarely seen, as it opens only in sunlight and soon withers.

Drosera breviflora
Sundew

Sundew is 1 of the 4 types of insectivorous plants in Texas, each of which has its own way of catching its prey. (The others are the small butterwort, floating bladderwort, and yellow pitcher plant.) The paddle-shaped leaves of the sundew form a rosette at the base, greenish to reddish and densely covered on the upper surface with hairs exuding a clear, sticky liquid which attracts and traps various kinds of insects. The more they struggle to free themselves, the more entrapped they become. The leaf folds over the insect and digests it by enzyme activity. If the leaf is unrolled, the skeleton of the insect will be found, just as one finds them at the bottom of the pitcher-plant leaf.

There are several flower buds at the end of a single, delicate stem, 4–5 inches tall, and they open one at a time. They have 5 pale pink petals, ⅜ inch long and almost round. They are most common in boggy, damp areas in Southeast Texas, although we have found a few on the north shore of Lake Tyler and a few in "Sheff's Woods," 10 miles north of Tyler, owned and managed by Nature Conservancy. Photographed near Saratoga in August. *East and Southeast Texas. April–June. Annual; sometimes biennial or perennial.*

ERICACEAE
Heath Family

The Heath Family consists of shrubs and
small trees. Leaves are usually alternate,
occasionally opposite, simple, entire
or finely and sharply toothed, and often leathery. Flowers are at the end of
branches or in the axils of the upper
leaves, solitary or in racemes, appearing
before the leaves in some species. The calyx is 5-toothed, the corolla 5-toothed or
lobed, with 5 or 10 stamens and 1 pistil.

Arbutus texana
Texas Madrone (Madrono)

The madrone is a fairly rare tree in Texas,
found in the Chisos, Davis, and Guadalupe
mountains. It grows to 30 feet tall, and its
most striking feature is the thin, pinkish,
smooth bark, which peels off in thin
sheets. The leaves are shiny, stiff, and
thick, 2–4 inches long. Clusters of urn-
shaped flowers, ½ inch long or less, white
to slightly pink, appear from April to September. The red fruit ripens from September to December, and ripened fruit can
frequently be found on trees that are still
blooming. It is a favorite bird food and is
heavily browsed by goats and deer; many
trees in the Guadalupes have been killed
by deer stripping off the bark completely
around the small limbs. These were photographed in the Chisos Mountains in
April and October. *Mountains of West
Texas. Blooms April–September; fruits
September–December. Perennial.*

Rhododendron canescens
Wild Azalea (Honeysuckle Azalea)

Wild azalea is a showy shrub growing
up to 8 feet tall. Leaves are alternate,
deciduous, clustered, 1½–4 inches long
and ¾–1¼ inches wide. They are firm and
thick, with a dark green upper surface.
The sticky, slightly fragrant flowers,
which bloom before the leaves are mature,
grow in whorl-like clusters. They are pink
(rarely white), trumpet-shaped, about 1
inch long, flaring into 5 petal-like lobes.
There are 5 stamens, 1–1¾ inches long,
that extend well beyond the petals, and a
pistil equal to or exceeding the stamens in
length. The plant thrives best in piney
woods. Photographed in the Big Thicket in
April. *East Texas. March–April.
Perennial.*

Rhododendron serrulatum
Swamp Azalea, Hammock-sweet Azalea

Swamp azalea is an erect, irregular
branching shrub, growing to 15 feet tall.
The leaves, clustered at the end of
branches, are 1½–3½ inches long and
⅝–1½ inches wide, deciduous, lustrous,
green on both sides, with short stems. The
sweet-scented flowers are white, with a
lavender tube slightly enlarged at the base,
1¼–1¾ inches long with 5 narrow, petal-
like spreading lobes. The 5 stamens are
extended. It blooms in mid-summer after
the leaves are formed. Photographed in the
Big Thicket in June. *Southeast Texas.
June–August. Perennial.*

EUPHORBIACEAE
Spurge Family

The Spurge Family is large and varied, usually with milky latex, and is most abundant in the Tropics. Important species are sources of rubber, tung oil, castor oil, manihot (which provides a staple food for many South Americans), and tapioca. The family also includes the ornamental poinsettia and the Chinese tallow tree.

Most spurge flowers are small and lack a corolla. Some also lack a calyx. Sometimes bracts are conspicuous (as in snow-on-the-mountain) and look like a flower from a distance. The stamen and pistil, usually 1 each, are in separate flowers on the same or different plants.

Cnidoscolus texanus
Texas Bull Nettle (Tread-Softly, Spurge Nettle)

Texas bull nettle is usually 1½–3 feet high with several stems from the same root system. The deep taproot enables the plant to thrive even in the hottest part of the summer. Leaves are alternate, 2–4 inches long, divided into 5 leaflets, crinkled in appearance and covered with stinging hairs. If one brushes against the leaves, one will feel the "sting" for 30–45 minutes. If any part of the stem is broken, a milky sap appears, and some people are allergic to this as well as the "sting" of the hairs. The flower consists of 5–7 white, petal-like sepals, united below; there are no petals. There are 10 or more stamens and a 3-lobed pistil. The fruit, or seeds, are clustered in 4 separate compartments held tightly together by the tough, almost round seedpod. It, too, is covered with stinging hairs. When the seeds mature, the outside "fleshy" part shrinks and exposes the durable shell that holds the 4 seed compartments. Photographed west of Canton in July. *Statewide in fields and pastures. March–July. Perennial.*

Euphorbia antisyphilitica
Candelilla (Wax Plant)

Candelilla has been important economically for half a century in the Big Bend area of Texas. A high-grade wax is produced by boiling the plant in large vats, which we have seen in process on the Mexican side of the Rio Grande. The wax has many uses, in making candles, soap, ointments, sealing wax, phonograph records, insulation material, shoe polish, floor polish, waterproofing, and lubricants. It also has purgative properties. The species name, *antisyphilitica*, was given because of its purported use in treating venereal disease.

Originally common over much of the limestone country in Brewster and Presidio counties, candelilla is still abundant in Big Bend National Park, where it is protected and not in danger of becoming extinct through removal of the plants. It prefers the same habitat as sotol and lechuguilla.

The plant grows less than 3 feet high, with pencil-like stems, branching near the base, erect and usually leafless. The small white flowers, deep pink at the base, $\frac{1}{16}-\frac{1}{8}$ inch across, grow near the tips of the stems. Photographed in Big Bend National Park in April. *Big Bend area. April–November. Perennial.*

Jatropha dioica var. *graminea*
Leatherstem (Bloodroot)

Euphorbia bicolor
Snow-on-the-Mountain

Snow-on-the-mountain grows 1–4 feet tall. Its slender upper leaves, 2–4 inches long, are green, edged with a narrow band of white. The lower leaves are alternate, grow close to the stem, and lack the white edging. They are 1–1¼ inches long. The numerous, inconspicuous flowers grow in terminal clusters. They are white, have no petals, and are either staminate (1 stamen) or pistillate (1 pistil). Clusters group together to form larger clusters surrounded by numerous leaflike bracts which are conspicuously white-margined, 1⅛–2⅛ inches long and about ¼ inch wide. This plant adapts well to both dry and moist areas, growing luxuriantly in the Big Thicket as well as on the dry plains of Central Texas. When the stem is broken it exudes a white, milky sap that is irritating to the skin of some persons. Photographed between Waco and Corsicana in October. *Central and East Texas. July–October. Annual.*

We have never seen the leatherstem growing except under adverse conditions when, in order to conserve water, it had shed almost all of its leaves. Normally this would not happen until frost. The leaves, when present, are 1–1¼ inches long, in clusters on short, lateral branches. The plant is 18–24 inches tall, with reddish-brown stems that are extremely flexible, almost impossible to break. The small, cream-colored flowers, ¼ inch across, supported by red sepals, grow in clusters at the end of the stems. Flowers are urn-shaped, flaring out into 5 tiny lobes. The staminate and pistillate flowers are on separate plants. It is said that if the plant is pulled up, it exudes a reddish liquid, causing it to be known as "bloodroot." The seeds are a favorite food of the white-winged dove. This photo was taken in the Big Bend National Park in April. *Grows along the Rio Grande from Del Rio west; fairly common in Big Bend National Park.*

FOUQUIERIACEAE
Ocotillo or Candlewood Family

The Ocotillo Family consists of shrubs
with erect, wandlike stems. The blades of
the primary leaves soon drop off, and the
petioles develop into heavy thorns. Clusters of secondary leaves later appear in the
axils of the thorns after rains. The flowers
are showy and are borne in long, terminal clusters. Each flower has 5 overlapping
sepals, a 5-lobed tubular corolla, about
10–19 stamens attached to the base of the
corolla, and 1 pistil. The only Texas representative of the family is *Fouquieria
splendens.*

Fouquieria splendens
Ocotillo (Devil's Walking Stick)

Many persons mistake the ocotillo for a
cactus, as it grows in the same habitat and
has so many thorns. It is a soft-wooded
shrub with wandlike stems branched at
the bottom and growing gracefully to 20
feet. Leaves are alternate and leathery, ½
inch long or more; when they fall, the
strong, durable petiole remains.

The plant adapts well to drought conditions, shedding its green leaves when under moisture stress. The stem then takes
over their function; but if the drought
continues and becomes severe, the stem
turns brown as though it were dead. Still,
it will produce its brilliant red, intricate
flowers, which give no indication at all of
the plant's struggle. It is quite attractive
and is used as an ornamental in arid areas.
The blooming period is best from April to

June, but with good rains, the plants will
bloom well into the fall. The flowers are
in dense clusters at the end of the stems,
with 5 sepals, 5 petals ⅝ inch long, united
below, and 10–17 stamens.

Ocotillo grows commonly on rocky
slopes west of the Pecos. If a stem is cut
and stuck in the ground it will root and
grow well. In Mexico we have seen them
used for living fences around the house
and yard; and in West Texas they are
sometimes used for walls in buildings, the
dead stems held together in an upright
position. Photographed in the Big Bend
area in April. *West Texas. April–July.
Perennial.*

FUMARIACEAE
Fumitory or Bleeding-Heart Family

Many botanists unite this family with
the Poppy Family. It has finely divided
leaves and bilaterally symmetrical
flowers. Petals are in 2 pairs, with one or
both of the outer pair having a sac, or
spur, at the base. There are 2 sepals and
6 stamens.

Corydalis curvisiliqua
**Scrambled Eggs (Golden Smoke,
Curvepod)**

This spring annual has erect stems 6–16
inches high with leaves cut deeply into
many sections. The flowers are pale yellow, about 1 inch long, with 4 petals. The
outer 2 petals enclose the inner 2. One
petal has a short, straight, saclike spur
at the base. Photographed in the Davis
Mountains in March. *Grows throughout the state but is more common in the
west. February–May. Annual.*

C. micanthra, a winter annual, is the
most common species in East Texas,
though it grows in South Texas as well. It
differs from *C. curvisiliqua* primarily in
the characteristics of the fruit. Another
species, *C. crystallina*, is found predomi-
nantly in North-Central Texas.

GENTIANACEAE
Gentian Family

The flowers of the Gentian Family may be large or small, usually with 4 or 5 corolla lobes (but sometimes as many as 12) spreading at the end of a tube which is so short in some that the lobes seem to be separate petals; or, sometimes, with a funnel-shaped corolla bearing relatively short lobes. The color may be white, greenish, pink, purple, or blue. The 5 stamens are attached to the corolla. Leaves are usually opposite or whorled, with a petiole and smooth margins.

The beautiful flowers of the Gentian Family make them suitable for cultivation in flower gardens. They make excellent cut flowers, too, as the flower remains fresh for 3 or 4 days after being cut.

Centaurium calycosum
Buckley Centaury

This attractive member of the Gentian Family grows from Central Texas west. It prefers moist places at altitudes under 4,000 feet, but we have seen it grow luxuriantly along the roadside between Junction and Fort Stockton, and in the Davis Mountains. It is a low-branching plant 8–12 inches tall, with little foliage, so that the numerous pink flowers grow in a tight cluster, like a bouquet or corsage. Leaves are rarely more than ½ inch long, the blossoms 1 inch across. It has an unbelievable number of buds which continue to bloom for days, even when picked. It would make a beautiful border plant in a garden. Blossoms are tubular with 5 star-like lobes and a small white "eye" in the center. We photographed this flower between Junction and Fort Stockton in July. *Central and West Texas. April–October. Annual.*

——————————————————

Another species, *C. beyrichii*, mountain pink, is rose-pink, smaller, and less common. *North and Central Texas. June–July.*

Eustoma exaltatum
**Bluebell Gentian (Western Blue
Gentian, Blue Marsh Lily)**

Eustoma means "open mouth," referring
to the large throat of the flower. There are
several species in Texas. The one shown
here grows in nearly all parts of the state
except the pine forests in the east and the
mountains in the west. It prefers damp
areas and seems to reach peak condition
on moist prairies, where it sometimes
grows in profusion. This one was photographed in the Big Thicket in September.
  The large, bell-shaped flowers, 2–3
inches across, have 5–7 bluish-purple petals, less than 1 inch long, which are constricted into a small tube at the base and
have prominent purple markings in the
throat. The plants are 1–2 feet high with
smooth, erect stems and branches. The
leaves are long and oval with pointed tips,
1–2½ inches long. *Statewide except pine
forests and mountains. June–September.
Annual.*

Nymphoides aquatica
Floating Hearts

Floating hearts grow from a short, thick
stem. The leaf stems are 10 inches long,
slender and purple. The leaf is rather
thick, spongy, prominently veined, pale
green above, usually purple on the underside. It is almost round, up to 6 inches
wide, and deeply cut at the base. The
flowers are white, about ⅝ inch across,
parted into 5 petals nearly to the base.
Few to several flowers, with 3-inch stems,
grow in an umbel from the stem of the
leaf. At first sight one would think this
was a water lily. We photographed this
group in Caddo Lake, near Jefferson, in
May. *Southeast Texas; less frequently farther north. March–August. Perennial.*

Sabatia campestris
Meadow Pink (Texas Star, Pink Prairie Gentian, Marsh Pink)

Meadow pink plants are low, 3–20 inches tall, with opposite leaves, ½–1¼ inches long and smooth. The 5-lobed flowers, joined only at the base, are 1 inch across. They are usually deep pink, but occasionally purplish-pink to white. There are star-shaped yellow markings at the base of the petals. The single, short-stemmed flowers grow from the axils of the upper leaves. The pistil in this flower lies flat in the early stages but becomes erect and prominent as the flower matures. Photographed in the Big Thicket in June. *Eastern half of state. April–July. Annual.*

Another species common to East Texas is *S. dodecandra*. It has 9–12 petals, rose-pink to rose-purplish, with flowers 2½ inches across. It is quite similar to *S. campestris*, but much larger; it does not have the star in the center of the flower. *Eastern half of state. April–July.*

Rose pink, *S. angularis*, is an erect annual, usually 1½–2 feet tall with many branches from the bottom to the top, but especially on the upper half. Stems are 4-angled and winged on the edges. Leaves are opposite, 1½ inches long and ½ inch wide, attached directly to the stem. The starlike flowers, one at the end of each stem, are about 1 inch across, pink or rose-colored, and have a yellowish "eye" with 5 points, all bordered by a red line. They have 5 lobes which are joined so near the base that they appear to be separate. The 5 sepals are united, ¾ inch long, forming a slender tube. The 5 stamens have yellow anthers. *Eastern third of state. May–October. Annual.*

GERANIACEAE
Geranium Family

"Geranium" is derived from *geranos,* "crane," and this family is so named because of the unusual fruit formed by the pistil. At maturity the 5 parts of the ovary, each containing a seed, separate. Each is attached to a slender part of the style, which either curls upward or coils spirally. First, however, the style forms a long beak like the bill of a heron or crane or stork. Flowers have 5 sepals, 5 petals, 10 stamens, and a pistil composed of 5 parts. They are usually purplish, but may be rose or white, ¼–2 inches across. Leaves are palmately (in *Geranium*) or pinnately (in *Erodium*) divided, cleft, or lobed.

Erodium texanum
Stork's Bill (Pine Needle)

The horizontal stems of this low-growing plant are 15 inches long or more. Leaves are opposite, ½–2 inches long, with 3–5 lobes, rounded and fine-toothed. The lower leaves have long stems. The purple flowers bloom in clusters of 2 or 3 and have 5 petals nearly 1 inch long. The stamens have prominent yellow anthers. The blossoms are sensitive to light, opening late in the day and closing in the morning, except when it is cloudy. Stems are gray, covered with short hairs. The beaks of the seedpod are 1–2 inches long. During low humidity the tip coils, but straightens again when the humidity is high. In this way the seeds are dispersed. Photographed in McKinney Falls State Park, near Austin, in April. *Most abundant in Central Texas, but extends westward to the Trans-Pecos and north to Oklahoma. April–May. Annual.*

— — — — — — — — — — — — — — — —

Pin clover (filaree or alfilaria) *E. cicutarium,* also has horizontally spreading stems, up to 20 inches long, slightly soft and hairy. Leaves are up to 4 inches long and are pinnately divided into segments.

The 5 lavender-rose petals are up to ½ inch long, slightly longer than the sepals, and rounded at the end. They are very fragile and fall off the day they open. It is a good forage plant on the range. While part of the plant is still blooming, it bears pinlike seedpods, 1½–2 inches long (from which it gets its common name), 4 or 5 being attached to 1 stem. As these mature they break loose at the tip and coil spirally. *From Central Texas to the Trans-Pecos and north to the Panhandle. January–May. Annual.*

HIPPOCASTANACEAE
Buckeye Family

Some botanists include the Buckeye Family in the Soapberry Family (Sapindaceae). It consists of large shrubs or small trees. Leaves are opposite, palmately compound, 5–9 leaflets on a stout stem usually as long as the leaf, 3–6 inches. Margins are mostly fine-toothed, glossy dark green above and whitish beneath. The terminal flower cluster is 6–10 inches long, with flowers ½–1 inch long, either red or yellow. Seldom more than 2 large brown seeds develop in the 3-lobed leathery capsule.

Aesculus pavia
Red Buckeye (Southern Buckeye)

Red buckeye is a handsome shrub with showy, spikelike clusters of deep red, funnel-shaped flowers. The flower clusters are 6–10 inches long, and the individual flower is 1–1½ inches long. The leaf is made up of 5 leaflets joined at a central point on a stem as long as the leaf. They are fine-toothed, glossy dark green above and whitish beneath. The seeds and young shoots are considered poisonous. Soap may be obtained from the roots and a black dye from the wood. Buckeye grows best in sandy soil. This one was photographed near Garrison in May. *Common in woods in East Texas; less frequently found southwest to Uvalde and along the Red River to Wichita County. March–May. Perennial.*

—————————————————————

The western or yellow buckeye, *A. arguta*, has leaves divided into 7–9 leaflets. *Grows along streams in western part of state. March–April.*

HYDROPHYLLACEAE
Waterleaf Family

In the Waterleaf Family, the leaves of some genera are borne singly or in a rosette at ground level. Those of other species are pinnately lobed, cleft, or divided. Sepals and petals are 5-lobed. The 5 petals are joined to form a funnel, bell, bowl, or narrow tube with spreading lobes. There are 5 stamens, usually longer than the corolla, and the pistil has 2 styles and 2 stigmas. Flowers are usually blue, lavender, or purple, but white flowers are also fairly common and a few are yellow.

Hydrolea ovata
Blue Waterleaf

The sprawling, sturdy blue waterleaf plant, which grows to 3 feet tall, is spiny and covered with rough hairs. Several stems grow from the base and are branched in the upper portion. Leaves are 1–2½ inches long and 1 inch wide, alternate, undivided, and unlobed. There is a prominent spine on the stem just below the leaf. Many flowers and buds grow in clusters at the ends of the stems. Flowers are bright blue or purplish, 1 inch across, funnel-shaped, opening into 5 broad petal-like lobes. The conspicuous purple stamens extend beyond the petals. Blue waterleaf tends to form large colonies around the edge of lakes, ponds, and streams, and may stand in water for weeks without apparent damage. This one was photographed south of Conroe in July. *Eastern third of state. June–September. Perennial.*

Nemophila phacelioides
Texas Baby Blue Eyes (Flannel Breeches)

This annual herb is 3–24 inches tall and grows best in moist, shady places. The flowers are blue or purple with a pale center, about ½–1 inch across, with 5 sepals, 5 stamens, and 1 pistil. There is 1 flower in the axils of the upper leaves on a slender stem ¼–½ inch long. Leaves are simple but deeply cut, divided into 5–9 segments and irregularly toothed. Photographed in McKinney Falls State Park, near Austin, in April. *Southeast and Central Texas. April–May. Annual.*

——————————————————

Nama hispidum is a West Texas member of the Waterleaf Family. In years when the rainfall is good, this ground-hugging annual, 4–6 inches high, seems to cover the earth with purple, but in dry seasons it may have only a single blossom, almost as large as the rest of the plant. The leaves are ½ inch long and have a pungent odor. The funnel-shaped flowers grow in crowded clusters at the ends of the several stems. They open into 5 petal-like lobes, ½ inch across, purple on the outer part but white in the throat, with yellow stamens. *West Texas. March–May. Annual.*

Phacelia congesta
Blue Curls (Fiddleneck)

There are many species of *Phacelia* in Texas. Some have larger flowers and differently shaped leaves, but all have the tightly curled flower head. It is a good clue to their identity, though some of the heliotropes and borages have curled flower heads also.

P. congesta grows to 30 inches tall and is branched only at the flower heads. The flowers are blue to lavender, at the top of the plant, in a tightly curled flower head that gradually unfolds as the numerous buds come into bloom. Each flower has 5 petals and 5 stamens. The purple-stemmed stamens spread widely after leaving the flower tube and are conspicuous with their yellow anthers. Leaves are alternate, with 2–7 blunt leaflets 2–4 inches long, and fine hairs. Does well in cultivation. Photographed near Marble Falls in April. *Central and Southwest Texas. April–May. Annual.*

IRIDACEAE
Iris Family

The Iris Family differs from both the Amaryllis and the Lily families in having 3 stamens instead of 6; it also differs from the Lily Family in having the ovary below the perianth. As in the Amaryllis and Lily families, there are 6 tepals colored like petals. Leaves in the Iris Family are distinctive, sometimes described as being "astride" the stem; they are folded lengthwise, embracing in the fold the stem and a younger leaf. Many ornamental plants such as gladiolus and crocus as well as the garden irises belong to this family.

Eustylis purpurea
Prairie Iris (Pinewoods Lily)

Growing from a corm, the prairie iris is 1–2 feet tall and is usually unbranched. It has leaves 1½–2 feet long by 1 inch wide. Most of them grow from the base and are conspicuously veined, clasp the stem directly at the base, and are folded (pleated) for most of their length. The flowers grow in a cluster at the end of the stem and open one at a time for several days in succession. They are cup-shaped to flat. The 3 outer tepals are spreading, about 1½ inches wide, light to deep purple; the 3 inner tepals are dwarfed, cupped or crimped, and usually a deeper purple. The inner portion of the tepals is yellowish, spotted with reddish-brown. This one was photographed near Palestine in April. *Abundant in the piney woods of East and Southeast Texas. April–May. Perennial.*

—————————————————

A similar species, but smaller in every respect, is the pleated-leaf iris, *Alophia drummondii*. Its 3 outer tepals are wide-spreading, pale to dark violet, whitish near the base with violet spots, broadly sharp-pointed at the tip. The inner 3 tepals are much smaller, ranging from deep purple at the base to pale violet on the tip. *East and Southeast Texas. April–May. Perennial.*

Iris giganticaerulea
Giant Blue Iris (Blue Flag)

The giant blue iris grows 3–5 feet tall and prefers freshwater marshes. The leaves are 30 inches long or less and 1½ inches wide; they clasp the stem near the base. The blue outer tepals, 3 inches long by 1¾ inches wide, are marked with a whitish patch with a prominent yellow center; they hang down and are called "falls." The blue, erect inner tepals are 3 inches long and are called "standards." This specimen was photographed in the Big Thicket in June. *Scattered widely over East Texas. April–June. Perennial.*

────────────────────────

Another East Texas species is the yellow flag, *I. pseudacorus,* which has escaped cultivation. It grows in large clumps to 5 feet tall, with erect leaves 3–4 feet long and 1 inch wide. Flowers are yellow with tepals marked with brown streaking. *East Texas. April–May. Perennial.*

Sisyrinchium sagittiferum
Blue-eyed Grass

Plants belonging to the large genus *Sisyrinchium* are distinctive, having narrow, grasslike leaves and wide-open, often yellow-centered flowers which close in the afternoon. There are many similar species in various parts of Texas, with the greatest diversity found in sandy woods and along the Gulf Coast prairies of Southeast Texas. Characteristics separating the species are often very fine, with some intergrades.

This species, common to East Texas, grows 8–12 inches tall, in clumps, on threadlike stems. Leaves are narrow, 4–6 inches long. The flowers are bluish to purple, occasionally white, with 6 tepals, ½–¾ inch across, and a yellow center. This photograph was taken near Athens in April. *East Texas. April–May. Perennial.*

KRAMERIACEAE
Rhatany Family

The Rhatany Family comprises only one genus, *Krameria*. The flowers are peculiar in having 3 upper stalked petals and 2 lower glandlike, fleshy petals. They are all smaller than the crimson or purplish sepals, which may easily be mistaken for the petals. There are 4 stamens, more or less joined. The fruit is a round bur containing 1 seed, densely covered with white down, from which rise delicate spines.

Krameria lanceolata
Prairie Sandbur

This is not the sandbur of the Grass Family (*Cenchrus* spp.); however, its burs are just as spiny, though densely covered with white hairs. The flowers and short silky leaves grow on prostrate branches, up to 2 feet long, from a thick woody root. The 5 wine-red sepals may be mistaken for the petals, which are smaller and tinged with green, the upper 3 being united. The flowers are about 1 inch broad. *Not conspicuous or abundant, but occurs in many parts of the Trans-Pecos. April–October. Perennial.*

—————————————————

Crimson-beak, *K. grayi*, is a densely branched shrub, 1–3 feet high, with purple flowers. The bark of the root is used by Mexicans in dyeing leather a reddish-brown. *Mountains of West Texas. April–September.*

LABIATAE (LAMIACEAE)
Mint Family

Plants of the Mint Family are aromatic, with square stems and leaves usually opposite and entire or lobed. Flowers are 2-lipped and irregular, with 4 stamens in pairs, 2 longer, or sometimes only 2; 1 pistil, 2-branched; and a 4-lobed ovary. This family includes mint, sage, rosemary, thyme, marjoram, lavender, and other herbs.

Monarda citriodora
Plains Horsemint (Lemon Beebalm)

Plains horsemint grows 1–3 feet tall with leaves up to 2½ inches long, sometimes lightly toothed. The green, leaflike bracts taper to a spinelike tip and bend downward. They are located under the clusters of flowers that surround the stem at intervals (typical of the horsemints). The 5 small petals are white or lavender, often dotted with purple. They are united to form a 2-lipped blossom 1 inch long with 2 stamens.

This species is less common than most of the horsemints. We found this one still healthy in late September (because of good rains) at 6,000 feet elevation in the Chisos Mountains. *West Texas. May–August; common May–June. Annual.*

Monarda fistulosa
Wild Bergamot (Beebalm)

Wild bergamot is an attractive member
of the horsemint group, growing 2–4 feet
tall. The slender stems are branched at the
top, each branch ending in a flower cluster
2 inches across, with lavender-pink flowers surrounding the stem. They are
2-lipped, 1–1½ inches long. The leaflike bracts which surround the flower
heads are often streaked with pink. The
leaves are opposite, up to 4 inches long,
with a few short teeth. They have a pleasant aroma and are sometimes used in fla-
voring tea. Photographed 4 miles west of
Canton in July. *East Texas. May–August.
Perennial.*

Horsemint, *M. punctata*, like other mints,
has square stems and is strongly scented.
The flower cluster is made up of very
small individual flowers with a whorl of
large, petal-like bracts, green to purple,
just under each whorl of blossoms. The
2-lipped flowers, ¾ inch long, are yellow
with brown dots. The upper lip continues
beyond the lower one, which turns downward and is broader. The plant is 1½–3
feet tall and the leaves are 1–3 inches long
and opposite. Alternating pairs of leaves
grow in opposite directions on the stem.
Statewide. June–September. Perennial.

Physostegia intermedia
Intermediate False Dragonhead
(Obedient Plant)

Flowers of the genus *Physostegia* grow straight up and down the stem on all 4 sides and at right angles to it. They may be moved laterally (like the pages in a book), and will remain in the new position; thus the common name "obedient plant."
The species shown here grows 1–5 feet tall. Its stem is square, solitary, and slender, usually unbranched. It prefers moist areas. Leaves are opposite, sparse, 2–3 inches long, and grasslike, but thicker than grass. Leaf margins are usually wavy. Flowers are lavender with purple spots and streakings, up to ¾ inch long, attached directly to the stem. They are 2-lipped with an inflated throat; the upper lip is unlobed; the lower lip is 3-lobed and spreading, with a broad middle lobe. There are 4 stamens. Photographed north of Palacios, on Highway 35, in April. *South Texas. April–June. Perennial.*

Another obedient plant, *P. digitalis*, grows to around 3 feet tall. The bell-shaped flowers, about 1 inch long, are pale lavender to pale pink, spotted with reddish purple. *Common over the eastern third of the state. June–August. Perennial.*
Blunt false dragonhead, *P. praemorsa*, is erect, 1–2 feet tall, with no branches in the upper part. Leaves are opposite, 1⅛–2¾ inches long and ½ inch wide or less. The larger leaves are on the lower part of the stem. The upper ones are sharply toothed. There are many large, showy flowers on the upper portion of the stems. Flowers are 1¼ inches long, pinkish-lavender, spotted with rose-purple. The 2-lipped blossom has 4 stamens and is inflated at the throat. This is the only *Physostegia* that blooms in the fall in its range. *East Texas. August–October. Perennial.*

Salvia coccinea
Scarlet Sage (Red Sage, Indian Fire)

Scarlet sage is an erect herb, unbranched to sparingly branched, softly hairy, 1–2½ feet tall, with a square stem. Leaves are opposite, simple, 2¾ inches long and 2 inches wide with a blunt tip. It is lightly scalloped to sharply toothed with a petiole 1½–2 inches long. There are 1–6 flowers in a whorled cluster at different levels, forming a raceme 2–9 inches long, with individual flower stems ¼–⅓ inch long and very fine. Flowers are scarlet to dark red, with 5 petals united to form a 2-lipped blossom, ¾–1 inch long, the lower lip notched; 2 stamens, 1 pistil. Photographed in Corpus Christi State Park in April. *Grows primarily in woods near the coast. March–August. Perennial.*

Salvia farinacea
Mealy Sage

Mealy sage is similar to *S. lyrata*. It is about 2 feet tall and is named for the mealy-white (sometimes purple) appearance of the sepals, which are covered with felted hairs. The blue flowers are 5-lobed and 2-lipped, ⅔–¾ inch long, with 2 stamens and 1 pistil. They have the usual sage fragrance. The long, narrow leaves grow in clusters, out of which grow the flower stems. The leaves may or may not have teeth. *Throughout much of Texas.* Photographed on the YO Ranch near Kerrville in May. *April–July. Perennial.*

Salvia lycioides
Canyon Sage

The canyon sage grows 2 feet high or more. Leaves are smooth, ⅓ to 1⅕ inches long, margins entire to finely toothed. Corollas are blue to indigo blue, 2-lipped, and opposite on the stem. Photographed on Lost Mine Trail in Big Bend National Park. *Found in canyons and rocky slopes of mountains in the Trans-Pecos. April– October. Perennial.*

Salvia lyrata
Lyre-leaf Sage (Cancer Weed)

Lyre-leaf sage grows 1–2 feet tall and has a rosette of leaves at the base. The leaves are deeply 3-lobed, with a few simple leaves higher up on the stem. This species has the typical square stem and 2-lipped blossom of the mints. The blossom is blue or violet, about 1 inch long. The 2-lobed lower lip is much longer than the upper, which has 3 lobes, the middle one forming a sort of hood. The blossoms are whorled around the stem. The sepals are purplish-brown. This specimen was photographed near Quitman in June. *Common in woods of East Texas. April–June. Perennial.*

Salvia regla
Mountain Sage

Barton H. Warnock has rightly called the mountain sage one of the most beautiful shrubs in the Chisos Mountains. It reaches its peak after most other flowers are on the wane, thus giving this attractive plant center stage. We photographed many of them at elevations from 5,000 to 7,000 feet in late September.

The plant grows 3–5 feet tall with several branches in the upper half. Leaves are alternate, ½–1 inch long, with scalloped margins and pointed at the end. They are as wide at the base as they are long. There are masses of crimson, 2-lipped flowers, about 2 inches long, at the ends of the stems. They last for several days. The sepals also are tinged with red. *Chisos Mountains. July–December. Perennial.*

Autumn sage, *S. greggii*, which grows 2–4 feet tall, is often cultivated as an ornamental. It is unbranched and has leaves 1 inch long and ½ inch wide clustered at the nodes on the 4-sided stem. The sepals are united, tinged with purple and strongly veined. The bright red blossom is 2-lipped, the upper lip extending forward, the lower one broad and drooping, the throat enlarged just above the opening. *West Texas. June–November. Perennial.*

LEGUMINOSAE (FABACEAE)
Legume, Pea, or Bean Family

The legumes are one of the larger families of flowering plants, including trees, shrubs, and herbs. In almost all Texas species the leaves are divided pinnately or palmately; in a very few species they are simple.

The flowers usually have 5 irregular petals. The upper one, called the standard, is generally wrapped around the others in bud, but spreads and turns backward as the flower opens and stands behind the others, often erect. The 2 side petals stand out as wings. The 2 lower ones, called the keel, are usually somewhat united and form a pouch which encloses the stamens and pistil. Usually there are 5 sepals, joined to form a cup or tube, 10 stamens, and 1 pistil. One subfamily, the *Mimosa* group, does not have the irregular flowers, but the regular flowers of this group have numerous stamens, giving the flower the appearance of a fluffy ball.

The characteristic that unites all members of this family is the legume fruit—a 1-chambered fruit that splits along 2 sides when mature (beans, peanuts). In this family are peas, clover, alfalfa, lupines, peanuts, indigo, wisteria, and many others.

Scutellaria drummondii
Skullcap

The many skullcaps in Texas can be distinguished from other mints by the crest on the upper surface of the blossom. Most of them have small, oval or rounded leaves, and all have bluish-purple flowers. *S. drummondii* grows up to 12 inches tall. It is often branched at the base, forming clumps. Leaves are opposite and densely arranged. Each leaf is ⅓–¾ inch long and mostly oval, occasionally somewhat oblong. Flowers grow in the axils of the leaflike bracts. They have 5 sepals and 5 bluish-purple petals united to form a 2-lipped blossom ⅔–1 inch long. The lower lip is notched. Photographed near Palestine in April. *Statewide. April–May. Annual or short-lived perennial.*

——————————————————

Another skullcap, *S. integrifolia*, grows 1–2 feet tall, is usually branched near the base and has erect stems. Leaves are opposite. Those near the bottom are often coarsely toothed, ⅓–1¼ inches long; upper leaves are untoothed, narrower, and up to 2 inches long. The purplish-blue flowers are ⅔–1 inch long on short stems that grow from the bract axils. *East Texas. April–May. Perennial.*

Acacia farnesiana
Huisache

The huisache that grows along the coast is shrublike, but in South Texas arroyos and creek bottoms it makes a spreading tree 20 feet tall or more. The pinnate leaves are twice compound, as often occurs in the Legume Family. The flower is round, almost 1 inch across, but the yellow petals are very short and almost concealed by the many stamens, which are also yellow. The flowers are quite fragrant and are worked heavily by honeybees, which make excellent honey from the pollen. Photographed near Raymondville in April. *Boquillas to Brownsville. January–April; flowers appear before leaves. Perennial.*
———————————————
Huajillo or guajillo, *A. berlandieri*, is a spreading shrub with many stems from

the base, growing 3–15 feet tall. The white-to-cream-colored flowers (yellowing with age), grow in ball-like clusters, ⅝ inch or more in diameter, and are quite fragrant. They have 50–100 or more stamens, but no petals. The pinnately compound leaves are delicate, almost fernlike, 4–6 inches long with 5–9 (sometimes up to 18) pairs of leaflets, and these leaflets are again divided into 30–50 leaflets. The flower is a source of heavy, light-colored honey, rated by many as the best in the state. The seed pods are 3–5 inches long and 1 inch or more wide. The seeds are a favorite food of the blue quail. *Coastal Bend and south to the Rio Grande. February–April. Perennial.*

Acacia rigidula
Blackbrush Acacia

Blackbrush acacia is a stiff, thorny shrub, growing up to 15 feet high, with many stems from the base. It often forms impenetrable thickets in Southwest Texas. The leaves are ⅜–1 inch long, divided into 2–4 pairs, ⅙–½ inch long, and each leaflet divided again into smaller leaflets. Flowers are white to light yellow, fragrant, in oblong clusters, 1–3 inches long, growing at the end of the stems. Individual flowers are very small, with 4–5 petals and many stamens, which are the most prominent part of the flower. The flowers appear before the leaves develop, April to May. It is an excellent honeybee plant. The aroma of the flowers can be detected as one drives down the highway even at the top of the speed limit. This one was photographed near Comstock in April. *Grows along waterways and arroyos from Del Rio to the Big Bend. April–May. Perennial.*

Astragalus mollissimus
Woolly Loco

Members of the genus *Astragalus* that are poisonous to livestock are called "locoweeds," while the harmless ones are called "milkvetches." The loco weeds cause a slow poisoning of horses, sheep, and cattle, but are especially harmful to horses, causing staggering and some paralysis. They have an unpleasant taste, fortunately, and animals have to be starved in periods of drought before they will eat them.

Woolly loco gets its name from the many soft hairs that cover its leaves and stems. The plant is 12–18 inches tall, with many sprawling branches that turn upward, forming a rounded clump. Leaves are 6–10 inches long, made up of 20–30 leaflets, thickly covered with silky hairs. The flowers are on the upper 2–4 inches of the stem and grow in clusters. They have 5 sepals and 5 lavender-to-purple petals. This photograph was taken in Big Bend National Park between Panther Junction and the Basin, in April. *From Central Texas to the Davis Mountains, but rare in the Chisos. April–June.*

————————————————

Giant milkvetch, *A. giganteus*, is a robust member of the milkvetch group, growing to 2 feet tall and slightly branched. The leaves are about 1 foot long with 20–30 leaflets 1 inch long or less. The plant is covered with short hairs. The pale yellow flowers are tightly clustered all around the upper 4–8 inches of the bare stem. The blossoms are 2-lipped, the upper lip slightly divided and standing straight up; the lower lip is 3-lobed. The 1-inch-long flower is attached to the main stem by a threadlike pedicel, ⅛ inch long. The sepals form a pale green tube that supports the blossom. *West Texas. June–October.*

Baptisia sphaerocarpa
Bush Pea (Yellow Wisteria)

The bush pea grows to 4 feet tall with many branches, rounded into a compact clump. It has large yellow flowers along the upper part of the stems, well above the foliage. Leaves are made up of 3 leaflets about 1 inch long. Some of the upper leaves may have only 2, or sometimes even 1, leaflet. The greatest profusion of this plant we have seen was near Alvin, where a 15-acre pasture was almost covered with it. This photograph was taken there in April. *East to Southeast Texas. April–May. Perennial.*

————————————————

Wild indigo or nodding indigo, *B. leucophaea*, grows in rounded clumps 12–18 inches tall. Its rather large yellow flowers grow in clusters on the upper 10–18 inches of the stem, bending slightly toward the ground, giving it its other com-

mon name, "nodding indigo." The leaves are alternate, 1½–4 inches long, divided into 3 distinct segments; but the stipules (leaflike structures that grow where the leaf is attached to the stem) are so large that they are sometimes mistaken for leaves. *Eastern third of state in open woodlands and pastures and along roadsides. March–April. Perennial.*

The well-known indigo blue dye is made not from this plant but from the genus *Indigofera*.

Several other species of *Baptisia* grow in East Texas, all with the same leaf structure, but the flowers may be yellow, cream-colored, white, or blue.

Caesalpinia or *Poinciana gilliesii*
Bird-of-Paradise

This South American plant is used widely
as an ornamental in the Southwest, but it
has long since escaped cultivation and
grows well in the Chihuahuan desert and
other parts of Texas. Its attractive flowers
bloom over a long period. Close up, it has
a mildly unpleasant odor. It grows 3–10
feet tall, occasionally even taller, and has
leaves 4–12 inches long, alternate and
compound. The 7–15 pairs of leaflets are
further divided into 7–10 pairs about ¼
inch long, and smooth.

The flowers have 5–7 yellow, spreading
petals, 1–1½ inches long, clustered on the
ends of the flower stems. The showy, yellow flowers have 10 long, brilliant red stamens protruding 3–5 inches beyond the
petals. This one was photographed near
Fort Davis in August. *Central and West
Texas. May–September. Perennial.*

Cassia fasciculata
Partridge Pea

When we tried first to get a close-up of a
single partridge pea flower a few years ago,
we discovered that all the flowers had 5
yellow petals of unequal size and irregular shape, about 1 inch across. The upper
petals have red spots at the base and the
lower petal is larger than the others.
Stamens are yellow. The pistil extends
conspicuously to the side opposite the stamens. The plant grows 2–4 feet tall, erect,
usually with a few branches near the top.
The leaves are alternate and have 8–14
pairs of small leaflets. Several buds grow
on a short stem between the leaves near
the top, but only 1 on each stem blooms at
a time. Photographed near Tyler in June.
*Abundant in poor or sandy soil in East
and Central Texas; spreads rapidly and in
some years covers large areas of uncultivated fields. Has a long blooming period,
June–October. Annual.*

Cassia lindheimeriana
Lindheimer Senna

Lindheimer senna grows widely throughout the Trans-Pecos. It grows to 3 feet tall
and has several branches. The compound
leaves have 4–8 pairs of leaflets that are
oval, sometimes pointed, and covered with
soft hairs. Flowers are bright yellow to
orange-yellow, about 1 inch across, and
clustered at the ends of the stems. The 5
oval petals are crimped at the edges. Photographed near Terlingua in October.
Trans-Pecos. June–October.

Another senna of Central and West Texas
is *C. roemeriana*, 1–1½ feet tall. It has a
5-petaled flower, 1 inch across, and compound leaves with 2 leaflets about 1½
inches long. One or more of the sennas
can be found in all parts of the state. They
vary in size, but all of them have the compound leaf and yellow flowers with 5
irregular petals.

Cercis canadensis
Eastern Redbud

Eastern redbud is a shrub or small tree, up
to 30 feet tall with a circumference up to
10 inches. It has large, heart-shaped leaves,
up to 3 inches across. The flowers are actually pinkish-purple, somewhat redder in
the bud. They are ¼–⅖ inch long, with 5
petals and 10 short stamens. They grow in
clusters and appear before the leaves.
When the plant is weakened by adverse
conditions, such as old age or drought, the
flowers grow along the main trunk and
large limbs. This is one of the earliest
shrubs to bloom in the spring. Photographed near Frankston in April. *East
Texas. March–April. Perennial.*

There are several varieties of redbud, differing mainly in leaf structure. *C. canadensis* var. *mexicana* grows in the mountains of the Trans-Pecos and east to
Crockett and Val Verde counties, blooming in March and April. All species are excellent for ornamental planting.

Dalea frutescens
Black Dalea

Usually grows less than 2 feet tall, hairless throughout, green leaves, red stem, magenta colored, pea-like flowers on a much-branched plant which is only partly shrubby at base. Grows in elevations 3,000–5,000 feet. The leaves have a fragrant oil when crushed. Photographed in Davis Mountains in September. *Especially Marathon Basin and Davis Mountains. June–October. Perennial.*

Dalea formosa
Feather Dalea

This dalea grows mostly 2–3 feet tall, rarely to 6 feet. Leaves are usually less than ½ inch long, 7–9 leaflets, glandular. The conspicuous hairy flower cups make this plant easily recognizable. Flowers are deep purple. Photographed in Davis Mountains in September. *Scattered throughout the Trans-Pecos region. July–October. Perennial.*

　　D. greggii, Gregg's dalea, is similar to *D. formosa.* It has short thorns and tiny, rose-purple, pea-like blossoms with a yellow beak. The greenish-gray color of the plant makes it look as if covered by a spider webb. Leaves have 3–7 segments. The plant is 3–6 feet across. It is a good honeybee plant and is often used in landscaping. *Sanderson to Candelaria. May–August. Perennial.*

Desmodium psilophyllum
Wright's Tickclover (Beggar's Ticks, Sticktights)

The little tickclover plant, so pretty in the spring, can become such a nuisance in the fall. The seeds are detached at the slightest touch and cling tenaciously to one's clothing by the numerous tiny, hooked hairs. The plant's several branches grow from ground level, 1–2 feet tall. Leaves are alternate, 2–3 inches long and half that wide. Flowers are at the tops of the main stems, on ½-inch flower stems. They are light to dark pink, ¼ inch long and 2-lipped. Photographed in Big Bend National Park, in September. *Mountains of West Texas, above 4,000 feet. May–October. Perennial.*

Erythrina herbacea
Coral Bean (Cherokee Bean)

The coral bean is found all over East Texas, and we have seen it as far south as Rockport. This specimen was photographed near Tyler, in May. It is a perennial shrub, usually under 4 feet high, with several unbranched stems. Leaves are alternate, scattered along the stem, 3 leaflets forming the leaf, which is triangular in shape and often prickly beneath. The leaves are 3–5 inches long and 3½–4 inches wide. The scarlet-red flowers, 1–2 inches long, often appear before the leaves, in spike-like clusters, on the upper portion of the stem. There are 5 united sepals and 5 petals 1½–2 inches long, with the upper petal wrapped around the other 4. The pod is blackish, constricted between the seeds, and up to 8½ inches long. One's attention is caught by the large, scarlet seeds, which are prominently displayed after the seedpod opens in early fall. The seeds are firmly attached to the pod by a sturdy ⅛-inch-long thread and will remain in place for months. This makes them excellent for floral arrangements, especially since the color does not fade. Children often string them for beads. These seeds are poisonous. The plant does well in cultivation. *East and Southeast Texas. April–June. Perennial.*

Lotus oroboides
Pine Deervetch

An inconspicuous little ground-hugging
plant, pine deervetch is about 1 foot across
with runners extending farther. It has
masses of bright yellow flowers, about ½
inch long and typical of the legume family. They turn reddish-orange, especially
on the underside, as they mature. They
are most attractive, especially considering
the plant's size and the fact that it is often
found where nothing else grows. Each
flower stem has 1–3 flowers. The leaves
have as many as 13 segments and may be
thin and pointed or thick and blunt. This
plant was photographed in Green Gulch in
Big Bend National Park, in April. *Chisos
and Davis mountains. April–September.*

Lupinus havardii
Big Bend Bluebonnet

Of the 3 species of *Lupinus* in Texas, *L. havardii* is the tallest, with the flowers well above the foliage. It grows best in the Big Bend area, where we have seen it blooming continuously from Shafter to Boquillas Canyon, over 100 miles. It was mixed with desert marigold, making both more appealing than either would be alone. In favorable years it covers the slopes and hillsides, presenting a magnificent picture against the desert background.

This bluebonnet grows to 3 feet tall, with the flowers on the upper 4–8 inches of the stem. They are deep bluish-purple, with a lemon blotch. Leaves usually have 7 leaflets. Like the other Texas species, it is a winter annual, which means that seeds should be sown in late summer for ornamental use. *L. havardii* blooms earlier than the other species. Photographed near Presidio. *West Texas. February–April; usually peaks in March. Winter annual.*

————————————

The tall stems and showy flowers of *L. havardii* distinguish it from *L. subcarnosus*, a smaller, less showy species, which was originally designated as Texas' state flower (in 1901). In 1971, however, the state legislature designated all *Lupinus* species as the official state flower.

Lupinus texensis
Texas Bluebonnet

The bluebonnet was adopted as the state flower of Texas in 1901, and in 1971 official state-flower status was extended to all species of *Lupinus*. *L. texensis* is the species most conspicuous in Central Texas. It grows extensively over the state, primarily from the northeast to the southwest and everywhere east of that line. It reaches its greatest floral display on the limestone hillsides of Central Texas, where it blooms from early March to early May. Large fields of bluebonnets, resembling a sea of blue, are not uncommon, especially around the highland lakes of Central Texas.

The plant grows 15–24 inches tall, with leaves usually consisting of 5 leaflets with pointed tips, joined at 1 point on a long stem. (Some have 4–7 leaflets.) As in all species, each leaf forms a little "bowl" that holds 1 large drop of water when it rains, giving the plant a shimmering, diamondlike effect. The densely clustered flowers bloom on the upper 2–6 inches of the stem. They are dark blue, 2-lipped, with 5 petals. The upper petal has a white center that usually turns wine-red or purplish as it ages. Photographed between Burnet and Llano, in April. *East, Central, and South Texas. March–May. Winter annual.*

Melilotus indicus
Sour Clover (Indian Clover)

Sour clover plants are 12–16 inches tall and bear little resemblance to the clovers (*Trifolium*). Leaves are alternate, divided into 3 leaflets. The yellow flowers are produced along numerous branches which grow from the same point on the stem as the leaf. The flower clusters are numerous, 2–3 inches long, and individual flowers are about ¼ inch long. The plant has the sweet fragrance of new-mown hay, especially when crushed. The new leaves are good in salads. Sour clover is valued as hay or forage, as a good soil builder, and as a honeybee plant. This one was photographed near Sinton in May. *From the coastal plains north; infrequently in the Trans-Pecos. April–September. Annual.*

Mimosa borealis
Fragrant Mimosa

Fragrant mimosa is a woody shrub 2–6 feet tall with round balls of pinkish-purple flowers, ½ inch in diameter, with 10 prominent stamens, and tiny, 5-lobed petals. The flowers gradually fade to almost white. Leaves are small, ¼–⅜ inch long, with 4 or more pairs of tiny leaflets. The plant has short thorns, about ¼ inch long. Barton H. Warnock reports this plant near Government Springs, not far from Panther Junction, in Big Bend National Park, June to October. We photographed this specimen between Kerrville and Fredericksburg in late April. *Perennial.*

Mimosa dysocarpa
Velvetpod Mimosa

Velvetpod mimosa grows 2–3½ feet tall
with many branches spreading widely
from the base. It has thorns in groups of 3
all along the 3-sided stem. The compound
leaves are alternate, made up of 16–20
leaflets which, in turn, have several
smaller leaflets. When touched, they close
like those of the sensitive briar. Large
numbers of the small flowers grow along a
short stem forming a 2-inch cylindrical
plume, consisting of 20–30 buds that
bloom at the same time. Flower heads are
composed of 3–8 such plumes clustered
on the end of each stem. They are slightly
fragrant. Photographed in the Davis Mountains in August. *Davis Mountains. June–
October. Perennial.*

Parkinsonia aculeata
Paloverde (Ratama, Horsebean)

The paloverde should be placed high on the list of ornamentals. It is a spiny shrub or small tree, as high as 30 feet, with long, graceful, slightly drooping branches bearing many long, delicate leaves and sprays of yellow flowers. The 5 yellow petals of the flower, ⅓–⅔ inch long, are almost equal, but 1 has a honey gland at its base and soon becomes red; it remains on the stalk longer than the others. The paloverde has a profusion of blossoms through the warm months, especially after rains. The seedpods are 3–5 inches long, narrow, and constricted between the seeds. The leaves are unusual. The leaf stem produces 2 stalks, almost parallel and 15–18 inches long, with 10–25 pairs of leaflets on each. The leaflets usually fall off during the summer, and the stems then carry on the function of leaves. Photographed near Alice in April. *Central and South Texas. April–May and sporadically until fall. Perennial.*

Prosopis juliflora
Honey Mesquite

In early spring the green, graceful leaves of the mesquite are among the most beautiful of all the springtime flora. Under favorable conditions it sometimes grows as high as 30 feet, but in drier areas it is a spreading shrub with long, thick roots which people sometimes dig up for fuel. Anyone who has ever sat around an evening campfire made of mesquite wood will be familiar with its long-lasting heat-producing qualities, as well as its inch-long spines. The hard wood is also used for fenceposts and sometimes even for railroad ties.

Leaves are alternate, deciduous, with long stems, made up of 12–20 leaflets about 2 inches long and ¼ inch wide, which are again divided into smaller leaflets. All are smooth, dark green, and linear. The flower stem is 3 inches long or more, containing numerous cream-colored flowers that honeybees seem to prefer. The long, white stamens are numerous, turning yellow with age. The beans, up to 8 inches long, gradually turn yellow and mature in August and September. They contain about 25 percent sugar and are a valuable livestock food. Photographed near Hot Springs, in Big Bend National Park, in May. *Statewide. May–September. Perennial.*

Robinia hispida
Bristly Locust (Standing Sweet Pea)

Robinia pseudo-acacia
Black Locust (Honey Locust)

Bristly locust is a much-branched, erect shrub, up to 8 feet tall, forming colonies from root sprouts. Stems and branches are stiff, hairy, coarse, and bristly. Leaves are compound, alternate, deciduous, and densely hairy, divided into 7–19 leaflets, 1½–2 inches long. Flowers are in clusters that hang from the leaf axil, dark pink to rose or orchid. They are 2-lipped, the upper lip shorter than the lower. This plant bloomed in our yard near Lake Tyler in April. *Common in East and Northeast Texas. April–July. Perennial.*

In East Texas the black locust tree grows 30–40 feet tall. The smaller branches have a pair of thorns at the base. Leaves are 4–8 inches long with 15–25 leaflets. The compact flower clusters are 4–6 inches long, white, usually drooping. Individual flowers are 1 inch long and quite fragrant. Photographed near Tyler in April. *Eastern third of state. April–May. Perennial.*

————————————————

Another locust species, *R. neomexicana*, which has clusters of rose-pink flowers and longer thorns, grows in far West Texas. *Guadalupe Mountains. May–July. Perennial.*

Schrankia uncinata
Pink Sensitive Briar (Shame Vine)

Sesbania drummondii
Rattlebush

The sensitive briar is a vine that sends several runners over the ground. They are usually 2–4 feet long and are densely covered with small prickles. Leaves are alternate, with 4–8 pairs of leaflets further divided into 8–15 pairs of tiny leaflets with prominent veins on the underside. The leaflets are sensitive to the touch; if one brushes against them or touches them, they immediately fold up against each other, suggesting the name "sensitive briar." They also close at night and in cloudy weather. The fragrant flowers look like small pink balls and grow along the stem at varying intervals. They have 4 or 5 sepals, 4 or 5 united petals, 8–10 pink or rose-purple stamens, and 1 pistil. This one was photographed south of Tyler in July. *East, North, and Central Texas; occasionally in the Panhandle. April–July. Perennial.*

There are several species in Texas, all similar in appearance. The yellow sensitive briar, *Neptunia lutea*, is also a member of the Legume Family and has oval heads of yellow flowers. *Eastern half of state. May–June. Perennial.*

The rattlebush is a rank-growing, woody plant 2–10 feet tall. It has many branches in the upper part, well separated, with few leaves, giving it a rather spare appearance. Leaves are alternate, 4–8 inches long on a short stem. They are divided into 20–50 leaflets, ½–1½ inches long and about ¼ inch wide. The yellow flowers hang in clusters about 2 inches long, on a thread-like stem about the same length. Each flower has 5 petals, the top petal being longer than the others and standing erect. When the seeds mature they are loose in the pod and rattle when shaken, suggesting the name "rattlebush." This one was photographed in the Big Thicket in September. *East Texas. June–September. Perennial.*

Sophora secundiflora
Texas Mountain Laurel

Texas mountain laurel is an evergreen shrub, usually 4–6 feet high but sometimes much higher. It has shiny, leathery, compound leaves, made up of 7–9 leaflets that are rounded on the ends. The dense clusters of violet-blue flowers have a strong scent, which some people find disagreeable but others like. There is considerable variation in the shades of color in the flowers, but all can be characterized as violet. The brilliant red beans that follow the flowers contain a poisonous alkaloid. Photographed at a roadside park 25 miles north of Hondo in March. *Grows from Central Texas to the Chisos Mountains and in the Davis Mountains. March– June. Perennial.*

————————————————

The Guadalupe mountain laurel, *S. gyposophila*, is no more than 4 feet tall but spreads to 15 feet across and has larger flowers than the Texas mountain laurel. *Guadalupe Mountains. May–June. Perennial.*

Neither of these is related to the southern mountain laurel, *Kalmia latiofolia*, which is a rose-flowered shrub of the Heath Family.

Trifolium incarnatum
Crimson Clover

The Texas Highway Department seeds the shoulders and medians of many major highways in East Texas with crimson clover. Although it does not grow wild in Texas, we have included it because many persons not acquainted with it may want to know its name. It presents an extraordinary display from late March to early May, peaking during April. The leaves are formed by 3 almost oval leaflets, rounded at the ends and tapering toward the base. The flower head is 2–3 inches long and cylindrical, blooming from the base upward. Individual flowers are about 1 inch long, crimson to dark red. The uppermost petal does not stand erect but is folded over the balance of the blossom, giving the flower head a compact appearance. This photograph was made near Mineola in April. *East Texas. March–May. Winter annual.*

Vicia dasycarpa
Purple Vetch

Purple vetch has escaped cultivation and grows along the highways and pastures of East Texas. It climbs and clings by tendrils and forms a dense, tangled mass, with many flowers and heavy foliage. The leaves have 5–10 pairs of leaflets. Flowers are abundant, growing from the leaf axil on a stem one-fourth as long as the flower cluster. The flowers, crowded on 1 side of the stem, are bluish-purple to reddish-purple 2-lipped blossoms ½ inch long. This photograph was taken 5 miles west of Canton in May. *Widely scattered over East Texas. April–June. Annual.*

Wisteria macrostachya
Wisteria

Wisteria is a trailing or high-climbing vine that is often used as an ornamental planting and has probably escaped from cultivation in many locations. We have seen it at old abandoned homesites where it filled several trees, making it look, at first glance, as if the trees were blooming. Leaves are alternate, 1¼–3¾ inches long, usually divided into 9 leaflets which are opposite on the leaf stem, with 1 leaflet at the tip. The flowers are in large, drooping clusters 6–9 inches long. Individual flowers are nearly 1 inch long and are lilac or bluish purple and quite fragrant. Wisteria grows in thickets, in woods, and along streams. This photograph was taken near Garrison in April. *Widespread in the eastern third of the state. April–August. Perennial.*

LENTIBULARIACEAE
Bladderwort or Butterwort Family

The Bladderwort Family consists of small herbs, growing in water or wet places, with a 2-lipped calyx and a 2-lipped corolla, 2 stamens with 1 anther and 1 ovary. The corolla is deeply 2-lipped, with the lower lip often 3-lobed, and with a prominent palate, spurred at the base in front; the palate is usually bearded.

Utricularia inflata
Floating Bladderwort

This insectivorous plant grows in freshwater marshes or shallow, sluggish streams, or in standing water in roadside ditches. It floats by means of hollow "ribs" that radiate horizontally from the stem at water level, or just below, always visible. From the center of these the erect stem rises up to 6 inches high and bears 3–14 yellow flowers ½–¾ inch across. From the "ribs" which sustain the plant in water grow large masses of fine, rootlike filaments on which are numerous microscopic bladders, from which the genus gets its name (*utriculus* means "small bladder"). These bladders have a complex and delicate mechanism for catching microscopic animals that brush against them. They are digested in the bladders and contribute to the nitrogen needs of the plant. Photographed on Lake Tyler in June. *From East Texas to the Gulf Coast. March–June. Perennial.*

Pinguicula pumila
Small Butterwort (Bog Violet)

Small butterwort grows 6–8 inches tall and is 1 of the 4 types of insectivorous plants found in Texas. (See also pp. 92, 215.) The few leaves form a rosette at the base of the plant and have a sticky surface that captures small insects. The margin of the leaf rolls inward over the insect until it is digested. There is 1 flower, whitish or pale violet, about ¾ inch across, funnel-shaped, somewhat 2-lipped, with 5 petal-like lobes and a spur at the base, like a larkspur. Photographed in the Big Thicket in June. *Grows in Southeast Texas; prefers moist, damp areas. March–June. Perennial.*

LILIACEAE
Lily Family

Plants of the Lily Family grow from bulbs
or rhizomes. The narrow leaves grow from
the base in most cases, sometimes
whorled or in pairs on the stem. Flowers
usually have 6 tepals, 6 stamens (only 3
have pollen), and a superior ovary.

The Amaryllis Family is very similar,
but its members have an inferior ovary.
Some botanists classify the *Yucca* and
Agave species in yet another family, the
Agavaceae.

Aletris aurea
Colic Root (Star Grass)

The colic root plant grows 1–3 feet high.
The thin leaves, 4–8 inches long, form a
rosette at the base of the stem. The flowers are tubular, yellow to orange and about
¼ inch long, 6-lobed at the tip. They form
spikelike clusters on the upper third of the
stem. This photograph was taken in the
Big Thicket in July. *East and Southeast
Texas. June–July. Perennial.*

Allium mobilense
Wild Onion

Wild onion is a common sight in the spring. Crow poison is similar and shares the same habitat, but the onion can be identified by its scent. It has a hollow stem 6–8 inches long and 3 or more basal leaves about as long and ⅛ inch wide. The flowers cluster at the top of the stem, individual flowers having stems ¼–1 inch long. The 6 tepals are rose-pink to white, fading with age. There are 6 stamens. Wild onions prefer open, unshaded areas, where they bloom during April and May. When rainfall is sufficient, they sometimes bloom again in the fall. This one was photographed north of Gilmer in April. *North and Northeast Texas. April–May. Perennial.*

Another wild onion, common to East Texas, is *A. canadense*, which grows 8–24 inches tall. It has 2 leaves, sometimes more, that are shorter than the flower stem. The flowers are in a round, compact cluster, 1–1½ inches in diameter. The 6 tepals are about ¼ inch long, white to lavender, fading with age. The plant grows from a bulb which tastes like cultivated onion. *East Texas. April–May. Perennial.*

Androstephium caeruleum
Fragrant Lily

This attractive little plant is unusual in that the leaves are much longer than the plant is tall. It grows to about 1 foot or less, but the smooth, gray-green leaves are often 12–18 inches long. The flowers have 6 tepals, which may be white, bluish, or lavender; they are partly joined to form a tube. The flower has a pleasant, spicy fragrance. This is an early spring flower. Photographed west of Canton in April. *Central and East Texas. March–April. Perennial.*

Calochortus kennedyi
Desert Mariposa

The mariposas are among the most beautiful wildflowers of the southwestern United States. This species is rare in Texas, but less rare farther west. The specimen shown here was growing under the most adverse conditions and was no more than 4 inches high; it has just 2 tiny leaves, saving its energy, perhaps, to produce the beautiful, normal-sized flower. To find a flower of such delicate beauty in such an unlikely place seems like a striking paradox, and gives one a genuine lift.

The desert mariposa generally grows to 8 inches high and is very conspicuous with its bright red-orange petals. The 3 petals are generally marked with black or dark purple near the base. It belongs to the same genus as the sego lily, which is more common in the southwestern states. We photographed this one between San Vicente and Glenn Springs in the Big Bend area in April. *April–June. Perennial.*

Anthericum torreyi
Crag Lily

The crag lily has a slender unbranched stalk, 1–2 feet tall. The leaves are clustered at the bottom. The flowers are ¾ inch apart around the upper third of the stem. They bloom from the bottom up. The 6 yellow tepals, each with a green stripe down the center, open out flat. They close in the afternoon and open again in the morning. This one was photographed in the Davis Mountains in August. *Mountains of West Texas. August–September. Perennial.*

Dasylirion leiophyllum
Sotol (Desert Candle)

The sotol produces an unbranched flower stalk 5–20 feet tall, with long, dense clusters of small white flowers on the upper third. The flowers are of one sex, male on one plant and female on another. At the base of the plant is a crowded cluster of ribbonlike leaves, 1–3 feet long and ⅓–½ inch wide at the base. They have spiny teeth along the margins that curve backward toward the base. In periods of drought, the round, cabbagelike base is sometimes cut up and fed to cattle after the leaves are removed. It is also a source of alcohol and is used commercially in the production of an alcoholic drink (also called sotol). Photographed in the Chisos Mountains in August. *Central to West Texas. May–August. Perennial.*

A similar species, *D. wheeleri*, is common in the Franklin Mountains near El Paso and blooms from June to August.

Erythronium rostratum
Dog-Tooth Violet

Hesperaloe parviflora
Red Yucca

The dog-tooth violet is actually a lily. It grows 4–8 inches tall on a bare stem that grows out of a pair of sturdy leaves that reach higher than the blossom. The leaves, 1¼–1½ inches wide, are smooth and shiny, with each side curved toward the center. The single blossom has 6 yellow tepals that curve backward toward the stem and are ¾–1½ inches long. The 6 stamens have brown anthers. This flower is fairly rare in Texas. Photographed in the Big Thicket in May. *Big Thicket (rare even there). February–May. Perennial.*

Red yucca grows 3–6 feet tall and rarely has a leaf or branch except right at the base. It has many stiff, narrow, sharp-pointed leaves at the base, with margins that become frayed and threadlike. The red flowers are scattered along the upper part of the stem and bloom from the bottom up. The petals form a tube ½–¾ inch long, fine-toothed at the opening, showing a tip of yellow on the inside. This plant is used widely by the Highway Department in landscaping, as far east as Austin. Photographed between Del Rio and Comstock in April. *Grows wild from Del Rio west. May–July. Perennial.*

—————————————
The dog-tooth violet resembles the glacier lily (*E. grandiflorum*), which blooms just a foot or so below the receding snow as it melts at elevations of 8,000 feet or more in the Pacific Northwest. We photographed it in Glacier National Park in August. The only difference a person would normally observe is that the anthers of the glacier lily are black, not brown.

Lilium tigrinum
Tiger Lily

This lily is an erect plant, 2–4 feet tall.
Small black bulbs are generally present in
the axils of the leaves. The blossom has 6
petal-like tepals, strongly bent backward,
red-orange with red-brown dots, and 6 conspicuous stamens with dark anthers.
There are 1–3 buds at the end of each
stem. Generally found on roadsides and
around old dwellings, the tiger lily is a native of eastern Asia. It is easily confused
with *Lilium michauxii*, which grows in
the same area. Photographed in the Big
Thicket in July. *Perennial.*

Muscari botryoides
Grape Hyacinth

Several species of *Muscari* are widely cultivated. Some of them have escaped and
are now wild. This one has flat leaves
growing from the base of the plant. The
stem is round and leafless; it grows 8–12
inches high. The beautiful, tiny, bell-like,
bright blue blossoms, ¼–⅜ inch across,
are tightly clustered on the upper 2–2½
inches of the stem. This plant is not
shown in other flower books as being in
Texas, but we photographed this one near
Tyler in April, and have found it elsewhere
in East Texas. *April–May. Perennial.*

Nothoscordum bivalve
Crow Poison (False Garlic)

Trillium sessile
Red Trillium (Wake-Robin)

This early spring flower is one of the first to appear on lawns, meadows, or roadsides throughout the state. Often it blooms again in the fall. It grows from a bulb and looks much like the wild onion, but has fewer and larger flowers on long stems and lacks the onion odor. The leaves are all at the base of the plant, about ⅛ inch wide, but often quite long, 4–15 inches. The white flowers have 6 tepals with a green to brown stripe, and 6 stamens. Individual flowers are ½ inch across and grow in loose clusters on stalks 8–16 inches tall. This one was photographed near Tyler in April. *East, Central, and South Texas and sparingly west to the Trans-Pecos and Panhandle. March–May. Perennial.*

Red trillium grows 6–12 inches high. It has no leaves but has 3 leaflike bracts growing in a whorl at the top of the stem, dark green, mottled with shades of lighter green. They are 3–4 inches long, 1½–2½ inches wide, and pointed at the tip.

Flowers have 3 sepals and 3 petals that are about the same size, but the sepals lie flat and the petals stand erect, ¾–½ inch long and ¼ inch wide. The sepals have a thin, yellowish stripe on the edges. The sepals, petals, and stamens are all essentially maroon-colored. Photographed 25 miles southeast of Woodville in May. *Southeast Texas. April–May. Perennial.*

Yucca torreyi
Torrey Yucca

Yucca is a genus of evergreen plants that includes many varieties. It is nearly impossible for the amateur to distinguish between the species. Some *Yucca* species have short stems, while others grow 20–40 feet tall and have woody, scaly trunks. The leaves are pointed, stiff, and narrow with sawlike or fibrous edges. They grow along the stem or in clusters at the base of the stem. The flowers have 6 tepals and are shaped somewhat like bells. Some are whitish-green, others cream-colored. They grow in a cluster on a stem which springs up from the center of a cluster of leaves. Some give off a strong fragrance when they open at night. The large fruits may be either fleshy or dry. They contain many small, flat, black seeds.

Many uses have been found for these plants. Rope, sandals, mats, and baskets are made from the leaf fibers. The buds and flowers are eaten raw or boiled, and the fleshy fruits can be dried and eaten. A fermented drink is made from the fruits. The roots and stems were used to make soap, some species being known as soapweed.

The Torrey yucca, shown here, sometimes reaches a height of 20 feet, but more commonly 3–10 feet. The trunk is often branched, but sometimes has a single stem. The flower head may extend to 2 feet on the upper portion of the stem. The flowers are bell-shaped, 2–3 inches long, creamy-white or tinged with purple, waxy, with 6 tepals, 6 stamens, and 1 pistil which is 1–1½ inches long. Leaves are 2–4½ feet long, straight and rigid, ending in a sharp spine 1½–2 inches long; they radiate around the stem. Photographed between Terlingua and Santa Elena Canyon in April. *Grows along the Devils River and west to Northwest Texas. March–May. Perennial.*

————————————————————

Beaked yucca, *Y. rostrata*, gets its com-

mon name from the shape of its fruit. It grows 6–12 feet high, treelike, with a trunk 5–8 inches in diameter. The trunk is usually unbranched. The leaves are narrow and stiff and grow in a radiating mass near the top; they are 8–24 inches long and about ½ inch wide in the middle. They gradually widen from the base to the middle, then narrow to a needlelike spine at the tip. The margins are horny, pale yellow, and more or less fine-toothed. *Confined to Brewster County. Perennial.*

Giant dagger yucca, *Y. carnerosana*, is rightly named, as the broad, large, fleshy leaves, with strong, needle-sharp points, are as lethal as a dagger. They are produced before the flowers in a rosette at the base of the plant. However, both the flowers and the leaves are produced on new growth each year, and therefore "rise with the stalk," as the flowers grow just above the pointed daggers. The plant grows to 20 feet tall. The greatest floral display we have seen produced by this yucca was at Dagger Flat in Big Bend National Park, between Persimmon Gap and Panther Junction in early April. One stalk weighed 70 pounds and had 1,000 blossoms. *Big Bend area. March–June. Perennial.*

Faxon yucca, *Y. faxoniana*, is commonly called Spanish dagger because of its daggerlike leaves. It is known to grow to 40 feet, but in Texas we have never seen one over half that high. The diameter increases with the height, from 8 to 24 inches. *High desert plateaus in Southwest Texas and in the Guadalupe Mountains. April–June. Perennial.*

Bear grass yucca, *Y. louisianensis*, grows 3–8 feet tall, with its leaves mainly at the base of the plant. They are about 2 feet long and ½–¾ inch wide, sharp-pointed, stiff but not rigid. The numerous flowers form a cluster up to 2 feet long on the upper part of the stem. They generally do not fruit due to the absence of the yucca moth. *Widely distributed over the state, preferring dry, sandy, or upland soils. April–June. Perennial.*

Zigadenus glaberrimus
Camas

This camas grows 2–4 feet tall and is
sparingly branched. The leaves, 12–16
inches long, are at the base of the plant.
The branches have 6–12 flowers growing
on short stems, or sometimes attached
directly to the main stem. Flowers have
6 tepals, off-white to pale yellow, 1 inch
across. The tepals lie flat, and the stamens, almost as long as the tepals, are
conspicuous. Photographed in the Big
Thicket in April. *Grows in damp areas in
Southeast Texas. March–May. Perennial.*

Zigadenus nuttallii
Nuttall's Death Camas (Poison Onion)

This common prairie flower grows 1–2
feet tall and has long, narrow leaves near
the bottom of the plant. The stout stems
grow out of a large, black-coated bulb,
which is poisonous, as are all parts of the
plant, even when dry. Sheep are often poisoned by it. Flowers are cream-colored, ½
inch across, growing around the top of the
stem in a round-topped cluster. The stamens have large yellow anthers. Photographed west of Bonham in April. *Northeast Texas west to the Edwards Plateau.
April–May. Perennial.*

Other species are found in East and West
Texas. All are poisonous.

LINACEAE
Flax Family

The Flax Family is small, but important because of the species of flax (*Linum usitatissimum*) which is cultivated for the fiber used in making linen and the seeds from which linseed oil is extracted. The word *linum* is Latin for "flax" and is the root for the English words "linen," "linseed," and "lingerie." The fiber is still called "line" in England.

Leaves are alternate with entire margins. Flowers usually have 5 petals, 5 sepals, 5 or 10 stamens, and 5 styles. Petals are very fragile. Flowers may be blue, white, yellow, orange, or red-brown.

Linum lewisii
Prairie Flax

Prairie flax grows 18–20 inches tall. It rarely stands straight up, but rather leans at an angle. Flowers are pale blue, with 5 petals about 1–1½ inches across, veined in darker blue. Each stem produces several flowers, blooming from the bottom upward. We have never seen more than 1 flower at a time open on any stem. The seeds are produced on the lower flowers while those above continue to bloom. We have seen several instances in which the wind had blown the flower off its stem and all the petals remained attached to each other with a hole in the center that had surrounded the stamens. If handled carefully, such detached flowers remain intact. The stem is leafy when the plant is young, gradually losing most of its leaves as it matures. Leaves are narrow and about ¾ inch long. Photographed on the Lost Mine Trail, in the Chisos Mountains, in late September. *Trans-Pecos. April–September.*

LOASACEAE
Stickleaf Family

The herbaceous plants of the Stickleaf Family include both annuals and perennials, with brittle stems covered with rough, bristly, or stinging hairs, and papery bark on the older parts. Leaves are alternate, simple, toothed or lobed, with short petioles or none at all. Flowers may be at the end of flower stems, single or in corymbs, or in headlike clusters. The tubular calyx has 5 slender lobes. There are 5–10 petals attached to the tip of the calyx tube, 1 pistil, and 5 to many stamens.

Linum rigidum
Yellow Flax

Yellow flax is common on the prairies of the Southwest. It is usually 8–18 inches tall, depending on growing conditions. It has a single blossom, 1–1½ inches across, on each of its few branches. Leaves are alternate, narrow, and ⅓ inch long. The 5 yellow petals have deep red centers from which grow the 5 stamens with yellow anthers. This photograph was taken between Brackettville and Del Rio in April. *East Texas; Central Texas from Del Rio north to Oklahoma. April–June. Annual.*

————————————————

Many species of yellow flax grow wild in Texas, the blossoms of all being very similar. Both *L. rigidum* and *L. imbricatum* are common in East Texas. The flowers of *L. imbricatum* are greenish to yellow, with red rays extending halfway to the top of the petals.

Eucnide bartonioides
Yellow Rocknettle

Yellow rocknettle can be found in the rock ledges all along the Rio Grande, including those on the trail to the historical Hot Springs (no longer operated) in Big Bend National Park, where we photographed it in early April. It is a striking flower, yellow, funnel-shaped, about 1¼ inches long and 2 inches across. One of its outstanding features is the many yellow stamens extending well beyond the rest of the flower, with a tip of yellow pollen on each stamen, giving it a delicate, graceful appearance. The bright, showy flowers open only in bright sunshine. Leaves are 2–2½ inches long, lobed and toothed in varying patterns. *Southwest Texas. March– November*

Mentzelia multiflora
Blazing Star (Prairie Stickleaf)

This plant, 2–2½ feet tall, has many branches and shiny white stems. It is noted for its rough, sticky foliage covered with hairs with minute barbs; hence the common name "stickleaf." The flowers, about 2 inches in diameter, open in the late afternoon and close in the morning. They usually have 10 yellow petals with many long stamens. Photographed near Fort Davis in September. *From the Panhandle to the Big Bend area. March– October. Annual.*

Other species of *Mentzelia* grow to 2½ feet high, with flowers 3–5 inches across and otherwise recognizably similar.

LOGANIACEAE
Logania or Strychnine Family

Many members of the Logania Family are shrubs or woody vines. The flowers are characterized by 4 or 5 joined petals and 5 stamens. The leaves are opposite, with entire margins and a minute ridge joining those of each pair around the stem. The superior ovary will distinguish this family from the Madder Family (Rubiaceae), which it superficially resembles.

Spigelia marilandica
Pinkroot

Pinkroot is rather rare in Texas, more common in Louisiana. It grows to 2 feet tall. Leaves are opposite, 1–4 inches long, tapering to a point. The flower clusters grow along the last 2 inches or so of the 4-sided stem, which is curved downward at the top. All the flowers grow on the top side of the stem. They bloom from the bottom toward the top. The flower is a narrow tube, 1½ inches long, ending in 5 petal-like lobes, yellow on the inside and bright red on the outside of the tube. The plant prefers moist woods. This one was photographed a few miles southeast of Woodville, in May. *Found along the eastern edge of the state, from Woodville to the Big Thicket and eastward to Louisiana. March–May. Perennial.*

Gelsemium sempervirens
Carolina Jessamine (Yellow Jasmine)

This high-climbing, many-branched, woody vine often climbs to the very top of pine trees in East Texas; from a distance, it may appear that the tree is in bloom. The leaves, about 3 inches long and half as wide, are opposite on short stems and are usually evergreen. The yellow, fragrant flowers, 1–1½ inches long and 1 inch across, grow from the leaf axils in clusters of 6 or fewer. They are funnel-shaped and deeply 5-lobed at the opening. This Big Thicket specimen was photographed in March. *East Texas. January–April. Perennial.*

LYTHRACEAE
Loosestrife or Crepe-Myrtle Family

Members of the Loosestrife Family include annual and perennial herbs, shrubs, and small trees. Leaves are alternate or opposite, simple, entire. Flowers are at the ends of flowering stems or in the axils, single or in whorls, spikelike or branched racemes. The calyx is cup-shaped or tubular, with 4–6 marginal teeth. The 4–6 petals are attached near the end of the calyx tube, lavender or pink to red, purple, or white, and slender at the base. There are 8 to many stamens.

Lythrum californicum
Purple Loosestrife

Purple loosestrife grows to 5 feet tall. The alternate leaves are about 1 inch long. There are 4–6 purple flowers, sometimes more, along the upper third of the stem. The sepals form a short tube for the blossoms, which open out into 6 soft petals, ¾–1 inch across. Photographed north of Corpus Christi in April. *Grows in moist soil, mostly in South Texas. April–October. Perennial.*

MAGNOLIACEAE
Magnolia Family

Members of the Magnolia Family are shrubs or trees. Leaves are alternate, usually closely bunched, simple, entire. Flowers are large, showy, single, at the end of a flowering stem, with many stamens. The calyx and corolla are colored alike, in 3 or 4 rows of 3's. The many pistils are crowded together, covering the receptacle, sticking to each other and, in fruit, forming a sort of fleshy or dry cone which contains the seeds.

Magnolia ashei
Ashe Magnolia (Deciduous Magnolia)

The Ashe magnolia is a small tree with a broad, round top. It has leaves 2–3 feet long and sometimes a foot wide. They are wider near the tip than at the stem, green on the upper surface and whitish beneath. The blossoms, which grow at the end of stout stems, are fragrant, creamy white, cup-shaped, opening out flat as they mature. Each blossom has 6–8 petals, up to 6 inches long and about half as wide, and pointed at the tip. The pistils form a fleshy, oval, seed-bearing cone which enlarges as it matures, 2–4 inches long and about 2 inches in diameter. The seeds are attached to the cone by slender threads. This magnolia is rare in Texas; we have seen only three, all in extreme East Texas, in Newton County. This one was photographed a few miles south of Newton in April. *April–June. Perennial.*

Magnolia grandiflora
Southern Magnolia (Evergreen Magnolia)

Many southern magnolia trees are simply magnificent, maybe 90 feet high, with limbs almost from ground level to the top. They have a dense growth of smooth, leathery evergreen leaves that are alternate, 5–10 inches long, shiny on top and rusty below. Fragrant, creamy-white flowers, which discolor easily if bruised, appear on the ends of thick, tough stems all over the tree. They are cup-shaped, about 8 inches across, with 6 thick petals, wider at the tip, where they are cupped. The blossoms open about 9:00 A.M. and close at night for 2 or 3 days; then all the stamens are shed and the flower reopens, turns brown, and disintegrates. The flowers produce conelike seedpods that contain large red seeds. When the pods open, the seeds often fall from their place and hang by silky threads. Children often use the seeds for beads. The tree is often planted in yards, but the leaves fall gradually throughout the year so that frequent raking is required. Grass will not grow well, if at all, under the tree. This one was photographed at Lake Tyler in June. *Eastern third of state. April–June. Perennial.*

Magnolia virginiana
Sweet Bay Magnolia

This swamp-loving shrub or tree grows to 30 feet high. Leaves are simple, green above and whitish below, 3–6 inches long and 1–2½ inches wide. This magnolia holds its leaves over winter and sheds them just before the new leaves form. The leaves are a favored food for deer and cattle and are browsed heavily in the winter when other food is scarce. The blossom is 3 inches across, opening in the morning and closing at night for 2 or 3 days. It has 8–12 petals and is very fragrant. This one was photographed in the Big Thicket in May. *Southeast Texas. April–June. Perennial.*

MALVACEAE
Mallow Family

Leaves of the Mallow Family are borne singly and in many species are veined palmately; they are lobed, cleft, or divided palmately. The flowers have 5 petals and 5 sepals. The distinctive feature of the family is that the numerous stamens have their filaments united into a tube surrounding the style of the pistil. The pistil is made up of several segments, each provided with a style and stigma, usually joined at the base. Some plants of this family are cultivated, such as cotton, okra, hibiscus, and rose-of-sharon.

Callirhoe digitata
Wine Cup (Poppy Mallow)

The wine cup is a perennial growing 8–20 inches tall, depending on moisture and soil, with gray-green stems. Leaves are alternate, basal leaves having stems about as long as the leaf; leaves are coarsely lobed or scalloped to deeply 5-lobed. There are few leaves on the upper part of the stem. Flowers have 5 petals, cup-shaped at first and opening out nearly flat as the flower matures. They are violet to red-violet, sometimes white, 1–2 inches across. The stamens and pistil form a conelike structure in the center of the flower. Photographed on Jim Bowmer's ranch, near Temple, in May. *Throughout East and Central Texas, southward to the Rio Grande; more rarely, northwestward to the Panhandle. April–late June. Perennial.*

There are several species of *Callirhoe* in Texas, varying in color: cherry-red, pink, and white. They bloom in widely differing areas and up to 3,000 feet altitude, but the blossoms are always recognizably similar. All are perennial.

Hibiscus lasiocarpus
False Cotton (Woolly Rose Mallow)

False cotton is so called because its flower closely resembles the flower of a cotton plant (*Gossypium*), which is in the same family. It grows 3–5 feet tall and has hairy stems and leaves. The leaves, toothed and alternate, have long stems, 4–6 inches. Stems are woody and somewhat brittle. The large white (occasionally pinkish) blossoms are 3–4 inches long, with a crimson eye at the center. The petals fold up at night and look as though they had never been open. We photographed this one in a bog just north of the Big Thicket. *Widely distributed over East Texas; prefers moist areas. July–October. Perennial.*

Hibiscus militaris
Halberd-leaved Rose Mallow

The halberd-leaved rose mallow grows to 6 feet tall with erect stems and leaves. The leaves are alternate and prominently lobed at the base, the lobes wide-spreading and sharp-toothed. Flowers bloom from the axils of the leaves, from the bottom to the top of the stem. The large cup-shaped blossoms, about 3 inches long, are pink, sometimes white, with maroon or purple throats. The 5 overlapping petals open by day and close tightly at night. Photographed southeast of Huntsville in August. *Swamps and damp areas in eastern third of state. July–August. Perennial.*

— — — — — — — — — — — — — —

Pale-face rose mallow, *H. denudatus*, grows 1–2 feet tall. Leaves are fine-toothed, 1–1½ inches long and almost as wide. The petals are ⅗–⅘ inch long, orchid-pink, with deep rose-red at the base. This is somewhat smaller than most flowers in this genus. *Trans-Pecos. February–May. Perennial.*

Malvaviscus drummondii
Turk's Cap (Red Mallow)

The Turk's cap gets its name from its resemblance to a Turkish fez. The broad, red
petals remain closely wrapped around one
another at the base but spread somewhat
toward the end. The stamens extend considerably beyond the petals. The flowers,
¾–1½ inches long, grow singly in the leaf
axils or, sometimes, in clusters at the ends
of the stems. The stems are erect, woody,
and widely branched. Leaves are alternate,
with stems 1½–4 inches long. The leaf is
3–5 inches long and about as wide, with 3
shallow lobes, coarse hair above, and a
velvety underside. The margins have shallow, rounded teeth. It grows 2½–3½ feet
tall. The red, apple-like fruit is about 1
inch wide and half as high. It ripens in late
summer or early fall, after the blossoms
disappear. Photographed near Tyler in August. *Abundant in East, Central, and
South Texas in open woods, along
streams, or in damp or shaded areas.
April–October. Perennial.*

Pavonia lasiopetala
Pavonia Mallow (Rock Rose)

Pavonia mallow has a rose-pink flower
that looks like a wild rose from a distance.
It has 5 petals, veined in deeper pink, and
is about 1½ inches across. The sepals open
out almost flat, and the blossom is
slightly cup-shaped. The leaves are in
clumps of 5–7, and the blossoms are on a
1-inch stem that grows from these leaf
clusters. Leaves are gently toothed, 1–2½
inches long and almost as broad. The
plant has several loosely arranged branches
and is somewhat shrubby. It is able to
withstand dry weather remarkably well.
Photographed north of Uvalde in late September. *South-Central Texas to the Rio
Grande. April–September.*

Sphaeralcea angustifolia
Globe Mallow

It is difficult to distinguish one species of globe mallow from another because of the slight variations that separate them. The flowers vary in color from lavender to salmon, red, and pale pink; this one is salmon-colored and is distinguished by its narrow leaves, 1–2 inches long, many of them folded in half down the middle, and all of them wavy on the edges. Normally it is 2–3 feet tall, but sometimes up to 6 feet. The flowers do not bloom regularly on the stem from bottom to top; new blossoms may appear high or low on the stem. The 5 petals are ½ inch long, and the flowers are cup-shaped. They usually bloom between June and November and may bloom more than once during that time if rains are favorable. We have seen them as early as the last half of April. They are abundant in the Davis Mountains, where this one was photographed in July. *Trans-Pecos. June–November. Perennial.*

MARTYNIACEAE
Unicorn-Plant Family

The Martyniaceae are herbs with chiefly opposite, simple leaves. The flowers have a 2-lipped calyx and deeply 2-lipped corolla. The lower lip of the corolla is larger, 3-lobed, and with a prominent palate, spurred at the base in front; the palate is usually bearded.

Martynia louisianica
Devil's Claw (Unicorn Plant, Ram's Horn)

This is a clammy annual herb, 1–3 feet tall, with large leaves, 5–inches across and up to 1 foot long, covered with glandular nectar which often collects sand particles. Flowers, 1–2 inches long, are purplish with yellow mottling inside. The plant is ill-scented.

The name "unicorn plant" refers to the remarkable fruits. These are at first fleshy, the flesh later falling away, leaving an inner woody shell tipped by a long, curved beak (the horn of the unicorn). The beak splits lengthwise, and the shell opens between the two parts of the split beak. These fruits are easily caught on the legs of deer, rabbits, and cattle or hooked in the wool of sheep by their spreading claws (thus the name "devil's claw"). The fruits are collected and used in nature crafts.

Photographed west of Comanche in August. *Occurs in scattered localities over much of state; most common in South-Central and West Texas. June–September. Annual.*

———————————————

Similar varieties of *Martynia* grow in other parts of Texas.

MELASTOMATACEAE
Meadow-Beauty Family

Plants of the Meadow-Beauty Family have opposite, prominently veined leaves with palmate, almost parallel veins, and variations in leaf margins. The flowers are often showy, with 4 or 5 petals and usually twice as many stamens. In Texas species, the stamens protrude prominently, and the petals tend to curve backward in most species. They vary in color: red, bright purple, pink, white, yellow, magenta, and violet-purple.

Rhexia lutea
Yellow Meadow Beauty

The yellow meadow beauty, usually about 18 inches tall, has many branches and flower stems growing out of the leaf axils of the 4-sided main stem. Leaves are opposite, 1 inch long and ¼ inch wide, and attached directly to the stem. They are slightly toothed, have a deep center vein, and are pointed at the tip. The yellow flowers, 1 inch across, grow out of the leaf axils on short stems which usually have one or more pairs of leaves. The 4 petals are almost round. The stamens are straight, lacking the curve of other species in this family. Photographed in the Big Thicket in May. *Grows commonly in moist pinelands of East Texas. May–June. Perennial.*

NYCTAGINACEAE
Four-O'Clock Family

Flowers of the Four-O'Clock Family lack petals but have brightly colored sepals which may be mistaken for petals. These are joined to form a perianth with 4 or 5 teeth or lobes. There are 1–9 stamens. The ovary base is tightly enclosed by the base of the perianth and appears inferior. Leaves are mostly opposite, with or without petioles, usually entire.

Rhexia virginica
Meadow Beauty

This meadow beauty is usually under 2 feet high, but occasionally up to 3 feet. Stems are 4-sided, with opposite leaves attached directly to the stems. Flowers are rose-pink to pale pink, with 4 petals almost as broad as long. The yellow anthers on the 8 stamens are conspicuous because the petals tend to fold backward. Photographed near Tyler in July. *Grows in low, damp ground in East Texas, from Wills Point to the Louisiana line and southward. May–September. Perennial.*

The purple-flowered meadow beauty, *R. alifanus*, has a shorter, broader leaf. *Widespread in moist pinelands in East and Southeast Texas. April–September. Perennial.*

Abronia ameliae
Sand Verbena

This beautiful flower which grows on the sandy prairies of South Texas is not, as the common name implies, a member of the Verbena Family.

The plants are 12–18 inches tall, branched and sometimes sprawling, and sticky or gummy all over. Stems are coarse and hairy. Leaves are opposite, 1–2 inches long and two-thirds as wide, and wavy on the edges with a stem ½–1¼ inches long. A flower stem grows out of each pair of leaves. The orchid flowers grow in umbel-like round clusters, 2 inches across with 40 or more individual florets. The florets are 1 inch long, tubular, with 5 petal-like lobes, each deeply cut and very delicate. There are 3–5 stamens. When the flower goes to seed it looks like a cushion filled with pins. Photographed 3 miles west of Falfurrias in March. *South Texas. April–August.*

A. *fragrans* closely resembles this plant and has a wider distribution. It is said to cover most of West Texas on plains and sandy hills.

Allionia incarnata
Trailing Four-O'Clock (Pink Windmills, Trailing Allionia)

The orchid-colored trailing four-o'clock is a vine that grows along the ground; the plant may be 10 feet across. The stems, leaves, and buds are covered with soft white hair. The stems and flowers are sticky, and one rarely finds a flower without grains of sand stuck on the upper surface. Technically, what appears to be 1 flower is a cluster of 3, but no one but a trained botanist would ever guess it. Photographed in the Big Bend area. *Dry, sandy regions of Southwest Texas. April–October. Perennial.*

A. choisyi also grows in West Texas and is very similar. However, it has smooth stems and the leaves are whitish on the underside.

Boerhavia linearifolia
Narrowleaf Spiderling

The many slender branches of the narrowleaf spiderling suggest its name. The
pale green stem grows 15–24 inches tall,
with thick leaves 1¼–2½ inches long at
the joints. The stem is brittle at the joints.
There are 1 or more spots between the
joints, maroon-colored and very sticky.
Eight to 12 blossoms grow at the end of
short flower stems, about ¼ inch apart,
mostly on 1 side of the stem. They bloom
from the bottom up, 3 or 4 at a time, and
are purplish-red, about ¼ inch across.
Flowers have a 5-lobed perianth formed
into a shallow tube; it opens flat and
is scalloped on the outer edge; 5 bracts are
found at the base of the perianth. As the
flower matures, the perianth lobes turn
backward, leaving the stamens protruding
prominently beyond the lobes. It is a delicate, dainty flower, widely spread over
spare limbs, giving it something of an ori-
ental touch. This one was photographed
in the Davis Mountains in September.
Grows in dry soil in West Texas.
June–September.

Mirabilis longiflora
Long-flowered Four-O'Clock

This plant grows up to 3½ feet tall. The
stem is heavy, brittle, and sticky, with several branches near the base. The leaves are
opposite. The lower leaves have stems 1½
inches long; the leaves themselves are
3–4 inches long. The upper leaves have
no stem and taper to a sharp point. The
branches and the flowers grow out of the
leaf axils. The flower stem has many buds,
but usually only 2 flowers bloom at the
same time on 1 stem. The slender tube of
the flower is 4–6 inches long, pinkish
with a red throat, spreading into a white
blossom ½–¾ inch across at the opening,
with 6 stamens extending almost an inch
beyond. The flowers bloom near the top
of the plant. This photograph was taken
on the scenic loop in the Davis Mountains
in September. *West Texas. August–*
September.

NYMPHAEACEAE
Water-Lily Family

The water lilies all have stems growing in
the soil under the water and long-stalked
leaves and flowers that float on the surface or stand above it. The leaf-blades are
round or oval, attached to the stalks in the
center or at a notch in the margin. They
have 3–6 sepals which grade into the 3 to
many petals and stamens and several simple pistils or a single compound pistil.
Flowers are white or pink.

Nuphar advena
Spatterdock (Yellow Cow Lily)

Spatterdock plants grow in shallow water
and are rooted in the mud. They have
large leaves, 4–16 inches across, that are
almost round except for the deep, narrow
cut a third of the way to the center, where
the stout stem is attached. Almost all of
the leaves lie on the water, some slightly
above. Flowers are 1–2 inches across and
held above the water by their stout stems.
They have 6 sepals, the outer 3 green, the
inner 3 yellow and petal-like. The yellow
petals are small, numerous, and stamen-
like, mixed with the many stamens. This
plant was photographed in Caddo Lake,
near Marshall, in May. *Widely scattered
over East Texas in bayous, lakes, and
roadside ditches. March–October.
Perennial.*

Nymphaea odorata
Fragrant Water Lily

The fragrant water lily is a rooted aquatic plant. The leaves have long stems and are bright green above and reddish or purplish underneath, almost round. They are narrowly and deeply cut almost to the center, where the stem is attached. They are up to 10 inches across, floating on the surface of the water or just beneath. There is 1 flower to a stem, white, fragrant, 2–6 inches across, and floating on the water. Flowers open in the early morning and close about noon. There are 4 sepals and many rows of white petals, often more than 25, which are ¾–4 inches long, thick, and pointed at the tip. There are more than 70 stamens. The outer ones are large and petal-like; they become smaller toward the center. This specimen was photographed between Athens and Tyler in July. *Throughout East Texas. March–October. Perennial.*

OLEACEAE
Olive or Ash Family

The Olive Family is essentially a family of trees and shrubs. In Texas there is 1 herbaceous genus, *Menodora*. The plants are low and somewhat woody at the base. Leaves have short stems or none and are very narrow or pinnately cleft into narrow lobes. The corolla is showy, with 5 or 6 spreading yellow or white lobes. There are 1 or 2 stamens. Ash, lilac, and privet are familiar woody members of this family.

Chionanthus virginica
Grancy Graybeard (Fringe Tree, Old Man's Beard)

We have photographed this lacy-looking tree in March and April from Jefferson to Beaumont, and west of Palestine. The one shown here was growing near Caddo Lake, in Harrison County. It grows up to 35 feet tall, usually less. Leaves are deciduous, opposite, 4–8 inches long and ¼ inch wide; the petiole is 1 inch long. The numerous delicate, fragrant, white-to-greenish-white flowers are composed of 4–6 strap-shaped petals 1 inch long by ¹⁄₁₆ inch wide. They hang in showy, branched clusters 4–6 inches long. Flowers open before or with the first leaves. *East Texas. March–April. Perennial.*

Menodora longiflora
Showy Menodora (Twinpod)

This species is named *longiflora* because
of the long, narrow tube of its flower,
which is 2–3 inches long. At the end of
the tube the 5 or 6 yellow petal-like lobes
flare out almost flat and are pointed at the
end. The stamens are hidden in the tube.
The plant grows 12–18 inches tall, usually
with several branches. Leaves are opposite,
narrow and smooth. We photographed this
one in the Davis Mountains in July. *Central and South-Central Texas, west to the
Trans-Pecos; prefers rocky soil in the
mountains. March–October. Perennial.*

ONAGRACEAE
Evening-Primrose or Texas-Buttercup Family

In the Evening-Primrose Family, the calyx, petals or petal-like lobes, and stamens are usually 2 or 4 each, though a few have parts in 5's; and the ovary is conspicuously below the other parts of the flower. Two genera are especially abundant in Texas: *Oenothera* (evening primroses) and *Gaura* (wild honeysuckles or bee blossoms).

The genus *Oenothera* is not difficult to recognize. Its flowers have 4 sepals (bent downward at flowering time), 4 petals, and (with 1 exception among Texas species) 8 stamens and a cross-shaped stigma. The ovary is inferior. Many of the most familiar species open near sunset and close the next morning.

The genus *Gaura* is composed of rather weedy plants, with leaves borne singly on the stems and frequently in a basal rosette. The flowers are in spikes or racemes, or are branching. They open in the evening. The 4 petals are on the upper side of the flower, giving it a slightly bilateral symmetry. There are normally 8 prominent stamens and 1 pistil; these are on the lower side. The stamens have reddish-brown anthers.

The genus is easily recognized, but the species are sometimes difficult, due partly to a great deal of hybridization.

Gaura suffulta
Wild Honeysuckle (Bee Blossom)

The genus *Gaura* is a distinctive group of plants with 4 petals on the upper side of the flowers and 8 long stamens and 1 pistil on the lower side. The anthers are reddish-brown. This species is a weedy plant 1–3 feet tall with many erect branches growing from the base. Leaves are 1–3 inches long, mostly at the base. Flowers are in spikes, opening from the bottom upward. They vary in color from white to orchid, deep pink, or red, usually turning red as they age. The stamens point downward. The flowers are called "bee blossoms" because their fragrance attracts honeybees. This one was photographed west of Sanderson in April. *From East Texas to the Trans-Pecos, and northwest to the Panhandle. March–August. Winter annual.*

— — — — — — — — — — — — — —

Scarlet gaura (*G. coccinea*) is 12–18 inches tall and one of the most fragrant species in this family. It is redder than *G. suffulta*, fading to pink, with long, red-tipped stamens. It grows throughout the Trans-Pecos and blooms all summer at elevations less than 4,000 feet.

Oenothera serrulata
Evening Primrose

Oenothera laciniata
Cut-leaved Evening Primrose

The cut-leaved evening primrose grows 4–18 inches high, erect or prostrate. Leaves are alternate, simple, pinnately cleft into rounded lobes, or sometimes merely wavy-edged or toothed. Usually they are about 2 inches long and ½ inch wide. The small, pale yellow flowers are borne singly in the axils, with 4 heart-shaped petals ⅕–⅗ inch long, 8 stamens, and 1 pistil. They have 4 pinkish sepals, united at the base to form a tube. Photographed near Fredericksburg in April. *Grows well in disturbed ground throughout the eastern half of Texas and westward to the Trans-Pecos and Panhandle. April–October. Annual.*

When you have become familiar with the yellow evening primroses, this one will attract your attention because of the black center and the black stigma. There is no other like it. It may have 1 or many stems up to 20 inches long, erect or tending to lie on the ground. The leaves are narrow, sharp-toothed, 2 inches long or longer. The flower tube is about ⅗ inch long, flaring out into 4 yellow, rounded petals up to 1 inch long. This one was photographed 10 miles west of Devine, in late April. *April–June. Perennial (may bloom the first year).*

———————————————

Four-point evening primrose, *O. heterophylla* var. *rhombipetala*, grows 2–3 feet tall. It is unbranched and heavily leafed from the ground to the flower cluster. Leaves are 3–5 inches long, decreasing in length as they grow higher on the stem. The flowers are bright yellow with 4 petals about 1½ inches long. The flower stems spread outward and upward with a cluster of blossoms at the top, forming long-stemmed clumps of flowers. *Abundant in Northeast, North-Central, and West Texas. May–October. Annual.*

Oenothera speciosa
Pink Evening Primrose (Showy Primrose)

The pink evening primrose grows 8–18 inches high. Leaves are alternate, 1–4 inches long. Flowers grow in a cluster at the ends of the branches. They are cup-shaped, up to 2 inches across, with 4 broad petals marked with dark pink veins. The center is greenish-yellow, to white at the base. Flowers are pink to rose-pink and occasionally white. The 4 sepals are united into a slender tube below the petals, but are pushed open and back as the petals open. We have photographed several acres of this species which had literally turned the countryside pink. This photograph was taken near Tyler in April. *Grows in great masses along roadsides and in open fields in East and Central Texas; rarely in West Texas. March–June. Perennial.*

ORCHIDACEAE
Orchid Family

The Orchid Family has been called the royal family of flowering plants, and is one of the largest in the world. Most of them are epiphytes, growing on the trunks of trees. They are numerous in tropical regions, but comparatively few grow in Texas and all are rare, with the exception of *Spiranthes*. None of the Texas species are epiphytes.

Orchids have 3 petals and 3 sepals and are bilaterally symmetrical. One petal, much larger than the others, is modified as a "lip," which serves as a landing for pollinating insects. In the center of the flower there is a column formed by the union of stamen and pistil. Most orchids have only 1 stamen.

Orchid roots require association with certain fungi, and the soil must be suitable for both. Many years' growth is required before an orchid produces a flower. The seeds are like powder, and only a few are able to germinate. Because of slow growth and strict growth requirements, many are endangered and need protection. One should never pick a wild orchid or, for that matter, any other wildflower that is not present in abundance.

Corallorhiza wisteriana
Early Southern Coral Root (Spring Coral Root)

Calopogon pulchellus
Grass Pink (Swamp Pink)

Calopogon comes from the Greek words meaning "beautiful beard." The prominent hairs, the beard, on the lip identify it. This species is a plant of moist areas and is most abundant in pineland bogs. It is known as grass pink because of the long, narrow, grasslike leaves. It grows 2½–4 feet tall, with 2 or more flowers arranged along the stem. The blossoms are rose-pink to pale orchid and are about 2 inches across. Photographed in the Big Thicket in May. *East Texas. April–June. Perennial.*

The orchids of genus *Corallorhiza* are among the few flowering plants that have no green color at any time, but support themselves, as mushrooms and toadstools do, on the dead remains of other plants in the soil. The stem is 15–18 inches tall, and the flowers are scattered along the top third. Flowers have 3 sepals and 3 petals, much alike; the lip is white, heavily spotted with purplish-brown, and curved sharply downward. This one was photographed in the Big Thicket in March. *Southeast Texas, on the edges of swamps and other moist areas. February–August. Perennial.*

The great coral root, *Hexelectris grandiflora,* is found in the Davis and Chisos mountains of Southwest Texas from June to October, characteristically under oak and madrone trees. It is about 12 inches high, and the flowers are rose-pink, about 1 inch across.

Other species of *Hexelectris* are found in North-Central and East Texas and grow on leaf mold in the woods.

Cypripedium calceolus
Yellow Lady's-Slipper Orchid

This orchid is easily distinguished from others by its large yellow lip, or slipper. It grows up to 2 feet tall and has large, strongly veined leaves 6–8 inches long and half as wide. It has a flower, sometimes 2, at the end of the stem, cream-colored to golden-yellow. Flowers have 3 sepals, greenish-yellow to brownish-purple, the upper sepal larger, usually erect, and hanging over the blossom. The upper sepal is 1¼–3½ inches long; the lower 2 sepals are united and appear as 1 beneath the lip. There are 3 petals. The 2 lateral petals are long and narrow, purplish-brown to greenish-yellow, and spirally twisted—the shoestrings to the slipper. The lip, or slipper, is creamy or yellow, and about 2½ inches long, and cupped to form the slipper shape. The stamens and pistil hang down toward the opening of the slipper. We have photographed these orchids from Caddo Lake to Burkeville. The photographs shown here were made southwest of Burkeville in May. *Rare in Central and East Texas. April–June. Perennial.*

Habenaria ciliaris
Orange-fringed Orchid (Orange Plume)

The orange-fringed orchid grows 2–3 feet tall and is easy to spot. The individual flowers, 1½ inches long, are dark orange to yellow-orange, with a conspicuous spur and a well-developed fringe on the lower lip. They form a tight cylindrical cluster on the upper 2–6 inches of the stem, which is as much as 3 inches in diameter. Leaves are alternate, attached near the base, 1¼ inches wide and up to 12 inches long. They are sharp-pointed at the tip, becoming bracts as they grow upward on the stem. We have photographed these orchids in Van Zandt and Harrison counties, though these photographs were made in the Big Thicket, in July. *Occurs in moist places and bogs in Southeast Texas and occasionally farther north. July–September. Perennial.*

Habenaria nivea
Snowy Orchid (Frog Spear)

The snowy orchid is a slender, erect, 1-stemmed plant that grows up to 3 feet tall. It has 2 or 3 leaves near the bottom, 4–12 inches long. The flower clusters are cylindrical, 4–5 inches long at the end of the stem and very compact, blooming from the bottom upward. Flowers are white, with 3 petals, the narrow lip at the top. The slender spur is conspicuous, ¾ inch long, extending to the side and curving upward. The snowy orchid often grows alongside the orange-fringed orchid in Big Thicket bogs and damp areas, where this one was photographed in June, though it is also found in other places. *Southeast Texas. May–August.*

Pogonia ophioglossoides
Rose Pogonia Orchid (Snake-Mouth Orchid, Beard Flower)

The rose pogonia orchid usually has only 1 flower on an erect, slender stem. It is rose- or pink-colored and, unlike most orchids, has a nice fragrance. The lower lip is densely bearded near the throat with white to yellow bristles. There is 1 leaf near the middle of the stem, 4 inches long or less and 1¼ inches wide. This one was photographed in the Big Thicket in April. *Commonly grows in bogs and wet pinelands in Southeast Texas. April–July. Perennial.*

Spiranthes cernua
Nodding Ladies'-Tresses Orchid

Of the half dozen genera of orchids in Texas, only *Spiranthes* can be classified as a common wildflower. Few people would guess that *Spiranthes* flowers are orchids, a fact that may help save them from collectors. The narrow, grasslike leaves are 8–10 inches long, growing from the base of the plant. The flowers are white and grow along the upper part of the slender, erect stem, which is 1–2 feet tall. They grow in 2–4 spiraling rows, forming a dense spike 6 inches long. The individual flowers, about ½ inch long, curve downward slightly, "nodding." The lip is about ½ inch long, with a flaring, crimped margin. This is one of the few orchids that have a fragrance. We photographed this specimen near Lake Tyler in November. *Found in bogs, meadows, and moist woods over most of East Texas. November–December. Perennial.*

There are several species of *Spiranthes* in Texas, many growing in less specialized habitats, making their range much greater. One of the most beautiful of all is *S. cinnabarina*, or cinnabar ladies'-tresses, which grows in the Chisos Mountains of Big Bend National Park, where it is found along small waterways and moist canyons. It has a spike of flowers 3–6 inches long that vary from orange to scarlet, and it blooms from August to November. Rare.

OXALIDACEAE
Wood-Sorrel Family

Plants of the Wood-Sorrel Family are small
with leaves divided palmately into 3 segments. The segments are often heart-
shaped and the leaves fold at night like an
umbrella. Flowers have 5 sepals, 5 petals,
10 stamens united by their filaments in 2
series, and a pistil with 5 styles. They
have a sour taste because of the presence
of oxalic acid.

Oxalis amplifolia
Large-leaf Wood Sorrel

This little plant likes the higher elevations, growing at altitudes of 4,000–6,000
feet, preferably under oak trees. Its few
leaves grow from the base of the plant,
with 3 leaflets about 1 inch long, notched
slightly at the center of the outer edge.
The leaves are cloverlike, about 2 inches
across, green above and below. They fold
downward, umbrella-like, at dusk or in
cloudy weather. Flowers grow in clusters
on leafless stems that grow from the base
of the plant. Only 1 or 2 bloom at a time.
They have a shallow funnel shape, ending
in 5 lavender-pink to purple petals. This
specimen was photographed at 6,000 feet
in the Davis Mountains in August. *Mountains of West Texas, 4,000–6,000 feet.
May–August. Perennial.*

Oxalis dillenii
Yellow Wood Sorrel

The name *Oxalis* is derived from a Greek word for "sharp," referring to the sour taste of the leaves. This plant grows to 15 inches tall and develops a deep tap root. Stems are usually erect. Leaves are palmately divided into 3 heart-shaped leaflets, green to yellow-green, which fold in the evening or when it is cloudy. The yellow flowers are ½–1 inch across, with 5 sepals, 5 petals, 10 stamens, and 1 pistil. There are 1 to several blossoms on a slender stem borne in the leaf axils. Photographed at Lake Tyler in May. *East Texas; blackland prairies in North and Central Texas. May–October. Perennial.*

Oxalis violacea
Violet Wood Sorrel

This is an erect, delicate plant up to 16 inches tall. The long-stemmed leaves grow from the base and at first are longer than the flowering stem. They are divided into 3 leaflets, gray-green to bluish-gray above and green to reddish-purple below, but similar in structure to those of *O. dillenii*. Like those of all wood sorrels the leaves fold downward, together, at night and in cloudy weather. There are 4–19 flowers at the end of each stem, lavender to pinkish-purple, the eye of the flower usually a deeper purple. The wide-spreading petal-like lobes are ½–¾ inch long. There are 5 petals and 10 stamens. Photographed near Austin in April. *Fields and open woods, usually sandy, throughout much of Texas. March–May. Perennial.*

PAPAVERACEAE
Poppy Family

Plants of the Poppy Family may be recognized by their sap: red or orange or yellow, sometimes white and milky. With few exceptions the leaves are borne singly. Before the flowers open they are enclosed by 2 or 3 sepals, which are pushed off as the petals expand. There are twice as many petals as sepals. The flowers are generally large and delicate, with many stamens and 1 pistil. The sap of some species is poisonous, the best-known one being the opium poppy; but the seeds of all species are used as food, and there is wide use of oil made from them.

Argemone chisosensis
Pink Prickly Poppy

We photographed this beautiful poppy between Castolon and San Vicente, almost in the shadow of the South Rim of the Chisos Mountains in April. The delicate flower is pale pink to lavender, 2½–3½ inches across, with 6 petals that are soft in texture and droop gracefully. The stems are prickly, as are the leaves on the underside. The leaves are lobed, especially the lower ones. *Plains and mountains of West Texas. March–December. Annual.*

————————————————

Rose prickly poppy, *A. rosea*, is one of the most attractive of the prickly poppies. The large, delicate flowers vary in color from pale pink to rose-purple and are more cup-shaped than the white-flowered species. They have the usual 6 petals. The gray-green leaves are blotched with white along the midrib and have slightly wavy margins armed with short spines. If the stem is broken it exudes an orange-colored sap. *From Central Texas to the Rio Grande. March–April. Annual.*

Argemone mexicana
Yellow Prickly Poppy

Yellow prickly poppy, 8–18 inches tall, has a smooth or slightly prickly stem. The deeply lobed leaves are a whitish green, and the upper ones clasp the stem between their two lower lobes. The upper surface of the leaf is smooth. Flowers are yellow, about 2½ inches across. Otherwise they are typical of the prickly poppies. This one was photographed between Del Rio and Brackettville in April. *Found along roadsides and in uncultivated areas over most of West Texas. April–October. Annual.*

————————————

White prickly poppy, *A. albiflora*, is the most abundant poppy in the state and sometimes covers large areas in a solid stand. It grows in most of Texas, but the heaviest concentrations we have seen were in the south-central part of the state, where we saw snow-white fields of 30 acres or more. The large, white flowers, up to 4 inches across, are cup-shaped to nearly flat, and bloom at the top of the stem. The 6 petals are circular with irregular outer margins. The numerous stamens are yellow. The 3 sepals end with a spine. If the stem is broken it exudes a white sap that turns yellow when it dries and is helpful in identifying the species. *Statewide. April–May. Perennial.*

Eschscholzia mexicana
Mexican Gold Poppy

When the Mexican gold poppy is growing in favorable habitats, it spreads over large areas and makes the earth seem as if it had turned to gold. It is closely related to the California poppy (*E. californica*). Its leaves are divided into many narrow, silvery-green segments. The flowers bloom at the end of the stems. They have 2 sepals that join at the top to form a cap, which is pushed off by the expanding petals. Stamens are yellow to orange. The flowers open only in fair weather, remaining closed at night and on cloudy days. This poppy is fairly rare in Texas. Barton H. Warnock has found them on the eastern slope of the Franklin Mountains and below Lajitas, on the lower trail across Mesa de Anguila. These were photographed northwest of Candelaria in April. *April– May. Perennial (blooms the first year).*

Papaver rhoeas
Corn Poppy (Red Poppy)

The corn poppy has escaped cultivation in Texas as it has in Europe. We photographed these near Austin in April. In Spain we saw it growing along roadsides and in rocky fields, sometimes up to 5 acres of nothing but poppies. We saw a man harvesting a poor stand of grain with a small hand-scythe, and he had more poppies than grain. The name "corn poppy" is appropriate, as Europeans refer to small grain as corn.

This poppy is a branching plant with leaves deeply cut and the edges usually toothed. The cup-shaped red flower, up to 2 inches across, has 6 petals, 3 inner and 3 outer, which are crinkled on the outer edges. *April–May.*

PASSIFLORACEAE
Passionflower Family

The Passionflower Family got its name from the early explorers, among whom were many priests, who saw in the flowers the crown of thorns of the crucifixion. This requires a pretty healthy imagination. Such extraordinarily complex flowers can stand on their own merits.

Principally vines climbing by tendrils, the plants bear alternate, petioled leaves and axillary flowers. The flowers have a fringed crown in addition to 5 sepals, 5 petals, 5 stamens, and 3 styles. The fruit is lemon-shaped.

Passiflora incarnata
Maypop (Apricot Vine, Passionflower)

The maypop is a vine that can climb over fences and bushes or run along the ground. The leaves are alternate, deeply lobed, looking almost like 3 leaflets. The flower is about 3 inches across. Its pollen attracts many insects. The fruit is oval and green, larger than a hen egg. When it ripens, the outside skin becomes light tan, deflated, and tough. The inside is edible and is sometimes used to make jelly. Photographed near Lake Tyler in June. *East Texas. May–August.*

—————————————————

Another passionflower, *P. lutea,* is similar, but smaller in every respect, the flower being only ¾–1 inch across, and greenish-yellow. The leaf is wider than long. *From East and Southeast Texas to the Edwards Plateau. May–September. Perennial.*

There are 3 other species of passionflower in Texas with differing leaf structure and flowers of different size and color, but the flowers on all of them have essentially the same intricate design.

PHYTOLACCACEAE
Pokeweed Family

The Pokeweed Family includes both annuals and perennials, sometimes with a
woody base. Leaves are alternate, simple,
and entire. Flowers grow in the axils, at
the ends of flower stems, or in leafless
racemes. The 5-lobed calyx is radially
symmetrical, small, and white or pink.
There are no petals, but several stamens
and usually 1 pistil.

Rivina humilis
Rouge Plant (Baby Peppers)

Rouge plant is a perennial herb about 1
foot tall that grows beneath trees and
shrubs. The flowers are about ¼ inch
across, white to pink, growing on the last
2–3 inches of the stems. The fruits are
numerous, red and almost translucent,
often appearing on the lower part of the
stem while the upper part is still blooming. They are a choice food for many kinds
of birds. The leaves are 1–3 inches long
and wavy on the edges. We photographed
this one in the Santa Ana Wildlife Refuge
in April. *Central Texas, south to the Rio
Grande and west to the Trans-Pecos.
June–October. Perennial.*

— — — — — — — — — — — — — — —

Another plant in this family, *Phytolacca
americana*, or great pokeweed, grows extensively in East Texas. It is a stout,
widely branched plant 4–9 feet tall, with
red stems and oblong leaves 4–12 inches
long. The flowers, about ¼ inch wide,
have petal-like sepals, no petals, 10 stamens, and 10 pistils joined in a disklike
ring. They are followed by dark purple berries on red stalks. The roots and seeds are
poisonous. *Grows at the edge of cultivated ground and in fencerows or recent
clearings. East Texas. July–October.*

POLEMONIACEAE
Phlox Family

Flowers of the Phlox Family have a united corolla that is bell-shaped or, more often, tubular with 5 spreading lobes. They often have an eye or spot of color at the throat. There are 5 sepals, 5 stamens, and 3 stigmas. The blossoms are often in clusters at the end of a stem, but some species have single blossoms instead. The leaves are varied in structure.

Gilia rigidula var. *acerosa*
Prickleleaf Gilia

It is surprising to come upon something as beautiful as this little gilia growing in a barren, forbidding environment. We found it near the Black Gap Wildlife Management Preserve in the Chihuahuan desert in August. It was not more than 4 inches high and had almost no leaves, with a blossom just over 1 inch across. The flower has 5 petals and is deep blue with a cream-colored center. The petals are united at the base to form a short tube, with lobes ⅓–⅝ inch long. There are 5 stamens and 1 pistil. Under more favorable conditions it grows up to 12 inches tall and has finely dissected leaves. *From Central Texas west to the Panhandle. May–October, depending on rainfall.*

G. *rigidula* is similar but slightly smaller, and the plant is widely branched, forming clumps a foot across. The numerous flowers are eyecatchers. *From Central Texas south and west to the Rio Grande. March–October.*

Ipomopsis longiflora
Paleflower Gilia

The range of the paleflower gilia is not
well known. The only 2 places we have
seen it are along the roadside east of Van
Horn, where it covered the ground for a
few miles, and at the foot of the Guadalupe Mountains. It grows 8–20 inches
high and is branched near the bottom and
also near the top, where each stem has
2–4 blossoms at the tip. Leaves are
threadlike and entire near the top, but
elsewhere they are sometimes divided into
3 segments. Sepals are ½ inch long, and
the flower tube is 1–1½ inches long and
quite narrow, opening out flat at the end
into 5 petal-like lobes, pale blue to white,
1 inch across. The tiny stamens extend
about ¼ inch beyond the petals. This photograph was taken on the right-of-way
about 20 miles east of Van Horn, in
September.

Ipomopsis rubra
Standing Cypress (Red Texas Star)

Standing cypress grows 2–5 feet tall. The
unbranched stems are pale green and very
leafy. The leaves are divided into 5–7
threadlike segments, reminding one of the
lacy cypress leaf. The bright red, tubular
flowers are more than 1 inch long and
have 5 spreading petal-like lobes. On the
inner surface they are pale orange-red with
dots of darker red. The flowers, which
resemble those of the cypress vine (*I.
quamoclit*), are closely clustered along
the upper part of the stem, those at the
top opening first. Often the plants form
large colonies and present a spectacular
sight when in bloom. This one was photographed near Tyler in July. *East and Central Texas. May–August.*

————————————————

A similar species, *I. aggregata*, is somewhat more spindly and not so heavily flowered, but otherwise much the
same. *Common in the Davis Mountains.
August–October. Biennial.*

Phlox drummondii
Phlox

There are many species of *Phlox* in Texas, and 1 or more can be found in almost any part of the state. It is difficult for the amateur to distinguish the different species, but fairly easy to recognize the genus. *P. drummondii* gets its name from Thomas Drummond, who gathered seeds of the plant near Gonzales in 1834. They were taken to England, where the plants grown from these seeds were named for him and became important in garden plantings. They were described as brilliant rose-red, with purple in some and darker red eyes in nearly all. Wild *P. drummondii* still grows in great profusion in the area where Drummond collected seeds. The color varies widely, from red to violet, pink, and white. The blossoms grow in clusters at the ends of the stems, 8–20 inches tall. The 5 sepals form a tubular shape for the blossom, but the petals lie flat and are wider at the tip. Stamens are inconspicuous. The flowers often form solid blankets of color in fallow fields, along roadsides, and in other uncultivated areas. These were photographed near Brenham in April. *East and Central Texas. May–October. Perennial.*

————————————————————

White-eye phlox, *P. mesoleuca*, has 5 sepals about ⅔ inch long, united to form a tube, and 5 pale-to-deep-pink petals. The petals, almost as broad as long, open out almost flat. The blossom is 1 inch across and has a white eye. Most species of *Phlox* we have seen are inclined to form large or small colonies, but this one grows in very small clumps and is often the only one in the area. It grows 3–12 inches tall, with narrow leaves 1–1½ inches long. *Scattered over the Trans-Pecos. May–October.*

POLYGALACEAE
Milkwort Family

The name "milkwort" comes from the be-
lief that cows or nursing mothers would
increase their milk supply by eating certain plants of this family. It should not be
confused with the milkweeds, which ooze
milk or sap from any cut surface.

The flower is small, intricate in structure, and bilaterally symmetrical. Of the 5
sepals, 2 are larger than the others and
petal-like, suggesting wings. There are 3
petals, partly joined to each other and to
the stamens, and smaller than the sepals.
Usually there are 8 stamens, united by
their filaments, and 1 pistil.

Polygala alba
White Milkwort

This is the most widely distributed species of *Polygala* in Texas. It has several
stems in a clump 1 foot tall or more.
There may be 1 or 2 circles of leaves near
the ground, but most leaves grow singly.
They are very narrow and up to 1 inch
long. The flowers are in dense racemes
and are white with a green center. Photographed near Presidio in April. *East,
South-Central, and Southwest Texas.
April–July.*

Polygala cruciata
Candy Root

P. cruciata requires moisture and is found primarily on the coastal plains. This one was photographed near Sour Lake in July. It grows up to 12 inches high and has few branches. The narrow leaves are in whorls of 4 Flowers are usually pink, occasionally white, and grow in a compact cluster, 1½ inches in diameter, around the upper 2–3 inches of the stem. *Southeast Texas and Coastal plains. July–October. Annual.*

Maryland milkwort, *P. mariana*, grows 6–16 inches tall and has no branches. The leaves are alternate and sharp-pointed. Flower heads are compact and rounded, but grow longer as the flowers open upward. The blossom is orchid to purple. *Grows in damp areas in the pinelands of East Texas. April–September. Annual.*

Bachelor's button, *P. nana*, grows 4–6 inches tall in small clumps. The flowers form a cluster around the end of the stem; the cluster is yellow, compact, and about 1½ inches long. *Grows best in moist piney woods or wet meadows in eastern third of state. April–June. Annual or biennial.*

Polygala polygama
Pink Milkwort

Pink milkwort grows 8–16 inches tall in the sandy soil of East Texas, usually in woods. Leaves are alternate, about 1 inch long and ¼ inch wide, attached directly to the stem. The erect stem has a slender cluster of pink flowers about ¼ inch long, loosely arranged on the upper part. It also has complete flowers growing underground, though they do not open. They are white. Using a round toothpick, we spent 20 minutes uncovering them in the sandy soil near Saratoga, where we made the photographs in May. *East Texas. April–June. Perennial.*

POLYGONACEAE
Smartweed, Knotweed, or Buckwheat Family

A distinguishing characteristic of the Smartweed Family is a leaflike sheath surrounding the stem, forming a tube at each leaf node. Leaves are usually alternate and simple, the flowers usually small, numerous, and in clusters. They usually have 6 sepals in 2 rows, often brightly colored. In some genera, the sepals are separate, but in others they may be joined to form a tube. There are 1–9 stamens and 1 pistil, which has 2 or 3 styles. Cultivated members of the family are rhubarb (*Rheum*) and buckwheat (*Fagopyrum*).

Polygala ramosa
Yellow Savannah Milkwort

Yellow savannah milkwort grows 12–18 inches tall, with leaves 1 inch long and ¼ inch wide. Flower clusters are numerous on short branches near the end of the stem, giving the plant a flat top of bright yellow. Flowers are less than ⅛ inch long. This one was photographed in the Big Thicket in June. *Grows in wet or damp areas of East Texas. May–September. Annual.*

—————————————————

Velvetseed milkwort, *P. obscura*, has orchid-colored sepals and petals a shade lighter. The flowers are no more than ⅜ inch across, growing alternately on the tiny stem. Like many small flowers, these have an intricate design, and a hand lens is necessary for detailed viewing. The plant grows 6–12 inches high with alternate leaves 1 inch or more long, smooth and slightly gray-green. *Mountains of West Texas. June–September.*

Eriogonum wrightii
Wild Buckwheat

Wild buckwheat is a woody shrub, 2–3 feet tall, with several slender branches. The whole plant is gray. At ground level it is surrounded by a thick mat of white, woody leaves about 1 inch long, but those along the stem are narrow and inconspicuous. The white, tubular flowers are in clusters, usually attached directly to the stem along the upper 2 inches, though some are scattered lower on the branches. Each flower has reddish sepals and bracts and a red stripe on the underside of the petal. In cool weather the flowers turn reddish-orange. The plants are found in association with juniper and sagebrush. This one was photographed in the Davis Mountains in September. *Abundant in West Texas. August–October. Perennial.*

— — — — — — — — — — — — — —

A related plant, smartweed, *Polygonum punctatum,* grows to 3 feet tall with leaves 2–6 inches long. The greenish-white flowers have sepals but no petals, are ¹⁄₁₆ inch across, and are in racemes 1–2½ inches long at the end of the erect stem. *Common in wet areas in Southeast Texas. May–October. Annual; sometimes perennial.*

Rumex hymenosepalus
Canaigre

The canaigre of West Texas has smooth stems and leaves and grows 1–3 feet tall. It is commonly seen in streambeds and gulches, though it is also found on well-drained high ground. The tuberous roots are rich in tannin. The large, fleshy, alternate leaves are often a foot long. The flowers bloom in large heads a foot long or more and are followed by large masses of pink-to-reddish-brown seeds, which are prettier than the blossoms. Canaigre is pretty in large flower arrangements. Photographed between Alpine and Terlingua in April. *West Texas. February–April. Perennial.*

— — — — — — — — — — — — — —

Curly-leaved dock, *R. crispus,* is erect and grows to 3 feet tall or more. It is easily distinguished from canaigre by the very fine, wavy margins of its long, rather narrow leaves. It is most common in sandy fields and uncultivated areas in East Texas.

PONTEDERIACEAE
Pickerelweed Family

The herbs of the Pickerelweed Family are smooth, without a rough or hairy surface, and grow in water or in marshes. Leaves are basal, simple, entire. Flowers are single or in spikes. Like those in the Lily Family, they have a perianth of 6 tepals, united in the lower part to form a slender tube. The flowers may be radially or bilaterally symmetrical. There are 3–6 stamens and 1 pistil with an inferior ovary.

Eichhornia crassipes
Water Hyacinth (Water Orchid, River Raft)

We first saw water hyacinths years ago, in Louisiana, forming blue ribbons through the countryside as they filled the bayous. They tend to grow so thick that they block water channels and constitute a hindrance to navigation. They grow best in sluggish streams or bayous, where they spread rapidly, extending their range. In shallow water they will root in the mud, but generally they are free-floating. Large sections often break away and are carried by the breeze or current to other parts of the stream, giving rise to the common name "river raft." Like many plants that are considered a nuisance, they present a beautiful sight when in bloom.

The flower spikes are 6–16 inches long, with many bluish-purple flowers that have a conspicuous yellow spot in the upper middle petal. The flowers are 1½–2½ inches long and about as broad, with 6 tepals, lasting a day or less. Photographed east of Batson in August. *Southeast Texas and as far north as Marshall and west to Kaufman. April–frost. Perennial.*

PORTULACACEAE
Purslane Family

The members of the Purslane Family are showy, fleshy, and supple. All are sun-lovers, and several annuals among them are garden favorites (moss-rose or portulaca, *Portulaca pilosa*, is one), although the flowers tend to be short-lived. They have 2 sepals, generally 5 petals, and from 1 to many stamens. Petals are mostly small but bright-colored, often in some shade of pink or lavender. The leaves are usually narrow and succulent.

Pontederia cordata
Pickerelweed

The large pickerelweed plant produces 1 spike of small flowers. The plant is often 3 feet tall, with long, heart-shaped leaves. The flower stem rises above the leaves except 1 leaf that grows behind the flowers. The deep blue flowers are on a spike about 6 inches long and bloom in succession from the bottom up, prolonging the flowering period for several days. This one was photographed southeast of Conroe in July. *Southeast Texas. June–September. Perennial.*

Talinum aurantiacum

Orange Flameflower

This is an erect, showy herb, 12–15 inches
tall, spreading at the base. Stems and
leaves are fleshy. The leaves are rather flat
and narrow, up to 2½ inches long, alternate, and attached directly to the stem.
Flowers, growing on short stems in the
leaf axils, are yellow to red-orange, with 5
petals ¾–1¼ inches long. They open in
the morning and wither in the late afternoon. This plant does best at elevations of
4,000–6,000 feet. Photographed near Fort
Davis in August. *Grassland plains of
the Davis Mountains. July–September.
Perennial.*

PRIMULACEAE
Primrose Family

In most families whose petals and stamens are of the same number, the stamens alternate with the petals. In the
Primrose Family, each stamen stands opposite the middle of a petal. There are generally 5 petals in Texas species, either
joined to form a distinct tube with flaring
lobes at the end, or joined only at the base
and thus appearing separate. There is 1
pistil with a single style, and there are 5
stamens. Leaves are divided and mostly
unlobed.

Anagallis arvensis
Scarlet Pimpernel

Scarlet pimpernel is the only species of
Anagallis found in North America. In
England it is known as the poor man's
weather glass, due to its habit of closing
its flowers at the approach of bad weather.
It is a low, sprawling plant, maybe 1 foot
tall, with many branches. The leaves are
opposite, just over 1 inch long, and attached directly to the stem. There is 1
flower to a stem that grows from the leaf
axils. Flowers are salmon to scarlet, ½
inch across. The 5 petals spread wide at
the opening and the stamens are prominent. As the flower gradually fades, the
petals turn backward a bit, so that the center becomes more prominent and is a deep
salmon color. This specimen was photographed between Galveston and High
Island on the upper Texas Coast in May.
*Sandy soils in South Texas. March–
November. Annual.*

RANUNCULACEAE
Buttercup or Crowfoot Family

Flowers of the Buttercup Family are usually radially symmetrical, but there are
a few exceptions, such as *Delphinium*,
which has bilaterally symmetrical flowers.
Casual observation shows little in common between the anemone and the buttercup, or the columbine and the delphinium, but when they are critically exam-
ined, the similarity is obvious.

Generally the flowers have 5 sepals and
5 petals. In some, the petals are absent,
but there are 5–10 sepals colored like petals. In distinguishing those that have
both sepals and petals from those that
have sepals only, care is necessary because
(1) sepals are often colored like petals, (2)
the sepals may fall as the flower opens,
the petals then being taken for sepals, and
(3) the petals in some genera may be small
and of unusual form. Flowers have many
stamens, and most have many pistils that
grow from a hump in the center. Each
flower grows singly at the end of a stalk
which rises among the leaves. A second
stem often grows from the same point
bearing leaves and a new flower stalk; and
this pattern may continue. Leaves grow
singly at the base of the flowering stem,
or, in some genera, they may be divided
into many small segments. Leaves on the
same stem sometimes differ in shape.

Anemone decapetala
**Southern Anemone (Windflower,
Granny's Nightcap)**

Southern anemone plants are 6–14 inches
tall, with 1 greenish-white or purplish-
blue flower to a stem. The few leaves are
well below the flower, often near the
ground. The parts of the flower that look
like petals are actually sepals, and there
are 10–20 of these. The pistils form a
conelike structure about 1 inch long. *A.
decapetala* is the most common anemone
in Texas and one of the earliest to bloom.
This one was photographed in Kerrville
State Park in March. *Widespread throughout most of state, especially in the limestone soils of the Hill Country. February–
April. Perennial.*

A similar species, *A. caroliniana*, is purple
and is restricted primarily to the sandy
soils of East Texas.

Clematis crispa
Curl-flower

Clematis pitcheri
Leatherflower

Curl-flower is a vine that may climb several feet on weeds, grass, or small bushes. Leaves are opposite, consisting of 2 pairs of leaflets. The pinkish-purple flowers grow on a naked stem and hang upside down. They have no petals, but the petal-like sepals are joined in a way that gives them the shape of an urn. They separate into 4 petal-like lobes at the rim, where they are wavy and crimped, curling backward and to the side. These beautiful flowers seem to do their best to conceal themselves by habitat and design, growing low and looking downward, but they are a rewarding "find" when one runs across them. Photographed near Sour Lake in April. *Southeast Texas. March–October. Perennial.*

——————————————

There are 3 or 4 other species of *Clematis* in Texas, and the sepals of all of them curl backward at the end. They vary in color from bluish to violet, to pink. *C. filifera,* growing in the Davis and Guadalupe mountains, is reddish.

Leatherflower is a delicate, twining vine. Leaves are opposite, divided into 3–5 pairs of leaflets that are marked on the underside by a prominent, raised network of veins. Flowers are nodding, on long, slender stems from the leaf axil. They are dull-purple to brick-red on the outside; dark purple, red, or greenish white on the inside. The 4 sepals are petal-like, thick, and united at the base; they are recurved or only lightly spreading near the tip; petals are absent; stamens many; pistils many. Photographed in the Big Thicket in May. *In thickets and edges of woods of East Texas, more common in southeast Texas. April–September. Perennial.*

Clematis drummondii
Texas Virgin's Bower (Old Man's Beard, Goat's Beard)

This is a climbing vine that covers fences and shrubs throughout the Trans-Pecos. Leaves are opposite and compound, with 5–7 leaflets ½–1 inch long, coarsely cut, sometimes toothed. The 4 petal-like sepals are light greenish-yellow, almost white, narrow and thin, with margins slightly crinkled, ½–1 inch long. There are no petals. Male and female flowers grow on separate plants. The stamens are quite conspicuous. When the seeds mature, the vine is covered with great masses of silky, feathery plumes, 2–4 inches long, which grow out from the seed cover. Photographed in the Davis Mountains in August. *From Central Texas westward through the Trans-Pecos. July–September.*

Delphinium carolinianum
Carolina Larkspur (Blue Larkspur)

The larkspurs are easily distinguished by the hollow tube that extends back from the uppermost sepal in the shape of a spur. The flowers of Carolina larkspur are deep blue, in a spikelike cluster 6–20 inches long on the upper half of the stem. The "showy" part of the flower is the sepals, which one is apt to mistake for petals; the actual petals are less conspicuous. The upper 2 petals also have spurs that extend backward within the spur of the sepal. The other 2 are bearded and deeply lobed. Photographed near Tyler in May. *Eastern half of state, with some extending into the Trans-Pecos. May–July. Perennial.*

————————————————

Another species, *D. albescens*, is the common larkspur of the prairies, and the greatest concentration of them that we have seen was in Northeast Texas on a large section of native virgin prairie, in April and May. They are taller and a bit coarser, and the flowers are white.

Ranunculus carolinianus
Buttercup

The buttercup is a creeper that roots at its joints and sometimes grows to 20 feet long. The roots are rather slender. The large leaves are divided into 3 leaflets 1–2 inches long and about the same in width. Flowers have 5 yellow petals that are ½ inch long and broader at the tip, with a shiny surface as though they had been waxed. The 5 sepals bend backward. This one was photographed just off the Trinity River on the western edge of the Big Thicket in March. *Along streams and ditches in Southeast Texas. February–April. Perennial.*

————————————————

R. fascicularis often overlaps with this species. It may be distinguished from *R. carolinianus* by the fact that the upper leaves are simple. The roots are also thicker.

Large-flowered buttercup, *R. macranthus,* grows 4–24 inches tall and has several erect stems with a few branches near the top. Leaves have 5–7 lobes and are supported on long stalks which clasp the stem. They are smaller and fewer as they advance upward. This is one of the most beautiful buttercups. The waxy yellow flowers, up to 2 inches across, have 8–18 petals, 3–5 sepals, and many yellow-to-green stamens. *Grows in damp soil in Central Texas, scattered places in the Trans-Pecos, and along the Rio Grande. March–April.*

Rough-seed buttercup, *R. muricatus,* prefers wet areas. Some species even grow in swift-running mountain streams. (*Ranunculus* means "little frog.") The flower stems grow in the leaf axils. The flower is about ¾ inch across, with 5 green sepals, 5 waxy yellow petals, and many stamens and pistils. It grows to 20 inches tall, usually erect, with many branches from the base and a hollow stem. Leaves are opposite and fleshy; the lower ones have stems 2–4 inches long. The leaf is 2½ inches wide and 1½ inches long and is deeply cut into 3–5 lobes. *East and Southeast Texas. March–May. Winter annual.*

ROSACEAE
Rose Family

The Rose Family is world-wide in distribution and is economically and aesthetically significant, as it includes not only roses but also apples, peaches, cherries, and strawberries, as well as many wildflowers.

Flowers usually have 5 sepals, 5 petals, and numerous stamens. Pistils may be several and separate or single and either simple or compound, and the flowers are mostly radially symmetrical. The base of the flower generally forms a cup, or saucer, upon which the perianth rests. Leaves are borne singly on the stem, generally with a conspicuous pair of appendages (stipules) at the point of attachment. The leaves are cleft or divided pinnately or palmately.

Fallugia paradoxa
Apache Plume

This shrub is conspicuous because of its size, up to 8 feet tall with many branches. It adapts well to desert conditions and is abundant in the Big Bend at elevations of 3,000–8,000 feet. It is browsed by cattle and goats. The flower is about 1 inch across, with 5 white petals and many stamens and pistils, blooming on long, naked stems. The plant gets its common name from the numerous reddish, plumelike hairs, 1–2 inches long, that grow out of the fruit. The evergreen leaves, up to ¾ inch long, are alternate and grow in small clusters. Apache plume grows rapidly with sufficient moisture and is often used as an ornamental. Photographed in the Davis Mountains in August. *Grows widely over Central and West Texas. June–August. Perennial.*

Potentilla recta
Cinquefoil

Cinquefoil grows to 2 feet tall and has
hairy stems and leaves. The leaves are divided palmately into 5–7 narrow, blunt,
toothed segments. Flower stems grow out
of the leaf axils and often branch 2 or 3
times, producing several buds which open
1 or 2 at a time. The flower, ½–1 inch
across, has 5 sepals and, alternating with
them, 5 bracts. It has several stamens and
pistils, and the latter form a conelike
structure in the center of the flower. The 5
pale yellow petals are heart-shaped. The
petals and the numerous stamens and
pistils may cause *Potentilla* to be mistaken for buttercups, *Ranunculus;* the 5
bracts are its distinguishing feature. Photographed east of Canton in May. *Northeastern Texas. May–August. Annual or
biennial.*

Rosa laevigata
Cherokee Rose

The Cherokee rose has 5 white petals forming a blossom 2–2½ inches across that opens nearly flat. It is a high-climbing shrub with thorny stems up to 20 feet long. The leaves are alternate, formed of 3, sometimes 5, evergreen, leathery leaflets. This native of China and Japan is sometimes cultivated as an ornamental. It often forms large bowers 10–40 feet long, completely covered with its snow-white flowers. Photographed near Saratoga in April. *Grows in uncultivated areas in woodlands; abundant in the Big Thicket. April–May. Perennial.*

Rosa setigera
Pink Prairie Rose

The beautiful pink prairie rose has climbing branches 6–15 feet long, with straight, scattered prickles along the stems. Leaves are divided into 3–5 leaflets which are sharp-pointed and 1–3 inches long. The 5-petaled pink flowers are 2 inches across, with many yellow stamens. They grow in clusters at the end of stems, but often open 1 or 2 at a time. They sometimes grow in bowers extending 8 feet high and 10–15 feet long. Photographed south of Bonham in May. *Eastern third of state. May–June. Perennial.*

RUBIACEAE
Madder or Coffee Family

The Madder Family includes herbs,
shrubs, and trees. Leaves are simple and
opposite, with margins entire. Sometimes
they may appear whorled when the stipules are as large as the leaf blades. Flowers
of Texas species are small, and most have
4 petal-like lobes, 4 sepals, and 4 stamens;
but these parts may occur in 3's or 5's in
some species.

Coffee beans and quinine are two familiar products from this family.

Bouvardia ternifolia
**Trompetilla (Scarlet Bouvardia,
Firecracker Bush)**

The red flowers of the trompetilla will
catch the eye quickly in the mountains of
West Texas. It grows 2–4 feet tall and has
many branches. Leaves are ¾–1¾ inches
long and grow in whorls of 3 or 4. The
scarlet flowers are 2 inches long and grow
in clusters of 4–12 erect blossoms. They
are tubular, separating into 4 short, petal-
like lobes at the end. Photographed in the
Chisos Mountains in July. *Mountains of
West Texas at elevations of 4,000–6,000
feet. July–September.*

Cephalanthus occidentalis
Buttonbush

Buttonbush is a shrub 8–12 feet tall with many branches. It usually stands in water, at least part of the time, or in very moist areas. The simple leaves, 2–8 inches long and 1–3 inches wide, are opposite or in whorls of 3, with prominent veins and rounded at the base. Flowers are clustered in ball-shaped heads, 1–1½ inches in diameter, with stamens protruding like pins in a pincushion. The trumpet-shaped white-to-yellowish flower is ¼–⅜ inch long, opening into 4 minute, spreading petal-like lobes. Each small flower has 4 prominent stamens. Honeybees work the flowers, and many birds eat the fruit. The bark has been used in the treatment of several types of illness. Photographed at Lake Tyler in August. *Common in East Texas; less frequent farther west. June–September. Perennial.*

Hedyotis nigricans
Bluet

The bluet is an attractive perennial adaptable to a wide variety of conditions, growing in nearly all parts of the state. It is a much-branched herb with stems 6–12 inches long. Leaves are simple, opposite. The flowers, about ¼ inch across, have 4 white to lavender-pink petals and are arranged in small clusters above the foliage. The bluet is always one of the early harbingers of spring, sometimes blooming in February, though the heaviest blooms are in March. This was photographed near Tyler in March. *Statewide. February– March. Annual.*

————————————————

Star violet, *H. crassifolia* or *Houstonia minima*, has purple-blue flowers ¼–⅓ inch across growing singly on the tips of fine branches. Each blossom consists of a narrow tube crowned by 4 lobes which spread sharply at right angles. The plant grows 4–6 inches tall with several branches. Though very small, star violets sometimes color a field blue. The opposite leaves are not more than ½ inch long, with the flower stem growing out of the leaf axil. *East Texas. March–April.*

SAPINDACEAE
Soapberry or Buckeye Family

The Soapberry Family consists of trees, shrubs, and, rarely, herbaceous climbers that have alternate and compound leaves, with leaflets entire, toothed, or lobed. Flowers often are numerous and small. There may be 4 or 5 petals—yellow, white, red, or purple; sometimes petals are absent. There are 4 or 5 sepals. Stamens are usually in 2 series, with some often reduced, giving the flower 8 or less stamens. It has 1 pistil.

Ungnadia speciosa
Mexican Buckeye

Beautiful clusters of purplish-pink, fragrant flowers appear before this much-branched shrub develops its leaves. The first time we saw it from the road, we thought it was redbud. The plant grows up to 10 feet high. Flowers have 4 petals and 7–10 stamens. The seeds are shiny, brown to black, and are considered poisonous. The flowers are attractive to honeybees. Photographed in Green Gulch in the Chisos Mountains in April. *Common in South and South-Central Texas and in the Trans-Pecos. Blooms March–August depending on rainfall. Perennial.*

SARRACENIACEAE
Pitcher-Plant Family

The Pitcher-Plant Family is represented in Texas by 1 species, *Sarracenia alata.* Its leaves, like those of other plants in this family, are hollow with an open, partially covered top. Water collects in these "pitchers," and insects are trapped, decomposed, and partially absorbed by the plant. Flowers hang at the tip of leafless stems, facing downward. There are 3 bracts, 5 sepals, 5 petals, and many stamens. The style has an extraordinary shape, like an umbrella upside down, with a stigma beneath each of the 5 angles.

Sarracenia alata
Yellow Pitcher Plant (Yellow Trumpet, Flycatcher)

The yellow pitcher plant is 1 of 4 species of insectivorous plants in Texas, getting part of its food from insects it is able to trap and digest. (See also pp. 92, 141.) It has 1 large leaf that forms a tube, larger at the top and sloping toward the base. The upper part of the leaf bends over the opening, as if to protect it. The inner surface of the leaf is covered thickly with tiny hairs that would make velvet seem rough by comparison, all pointing downward. The top part of the leaf has many small glands that exude a nectar that attracts insects. When they come in for a meal and touch the side of the tube, they literally hit the skids and go to the bottom, where the plant secretes a liquid that dissolves the soft parts of their bodies and absorbs them. We have cut these tubular leaves open and counted the skeletons, which have varied from 28 to 45; their odor was distinctly unpleasant.

The flowers hang their heads and look directly at the ground. One has to turn their faces up to see what they look like; but they are nonetheless attractive, with 5 sepals and 5 petals, yellowish-green to light orange and 1½ inches across. These

photographs were taken in the Big Thicket, ¼ mile off Village Creek, in Hardin County, in April. *Southeast Texas in damp, boggy areas. March–April. Perennial.*

SCROPHULARIACEAE
Figwort, Snapdragon, or Foxglove
Family

Leaves of plants in the Figwort Family are whorled, opposite, or alternate. The flower has 5 petals, joined to form a 2-lipped blossom. Some species have a "palate," an elevated part of the lower lip, which closes the opening between the lips. In some species there is very little difference between the upper and lower petals. Flowers in most species have 4 stamens, but those in the genus *Penstemon* have 5.

Agalinis purpurea
Gerardia

Gerardia is a fine-stemmed, woody, sprawling plant, almost vinelike, growing to 4 feet or more. It has several branches in the upper part. Flowers are pink to orchid, funnel-shaped, 1¼ inches long and 1 inch across, opening into 5 broad, flat, petal-like lobes with purple spots and yellow lines in the throat. Photographed in the Big Thicket National Biological Preserve in September. *Gulf Coast and Big Thicket. July–September. Annual.*

There are several species of this plant that differ only in minute details.

Aureolaria grandiflora
False Foxglove

The false foxglove is named for its narrow, bell-shaped blossoms, which resemble those of the foxglove, *Digitalis*. It is a somewhat sprawling plant, growing to 5 feet tall, usually lower. Stems are often single, sometimes several from the base, slender, much-branched. Stems and leaves are smooth; leaves lack teeth or lobes (except perhaps the lower ones), and they taper to a sharp point. The flowers are 1⅕–1½ inches long on flower stems ⅛ inch long or more. The yellow bell flares into 5 almost equal lobes, the upper 2 joined for over half their length; the lower lip is 3-lobed. The plant grows as a parasite on oak trees along streams and in marshy areas. This one was photographed near Edom, in Van Zandt County, in August. *Sandy open oak woods in East Texas. July–October. Perennial.*

Castilleja indivisa
Scarlet Paintbrush (Indian Paintbrush)

Scarlet paintbrush presents one of Texas' most beautiful landscape displays. In bluebonnet country, large fields of red and blue, sometimes mixed with white prickly poppy, are an impressive sight.

The paintbrush plant grows 6–15 inches tall. Leaves are 1–4 inches long, alternate, simple, with plain or sometimes wavy margins. Flowers with the attending floral leaves, called bracts, grow around the upper 2–7 inches of the stem. The intense red-orange color is due to the bracts, which almost hide the inconspicuous cream-colored flowers. Photographed in Northeast Texas in May. *Common in sandy soil from Northeast to Southwest Texas. March–May (best in April). Annual.*

Castilleja sessiliflora
Downy Paintbrush

Downy paintbrush grows 6–10 inches tall and often has several stems. The flowers are yellow-green, but the petal-like bracts, which are the most obvious part of all paintbrushes, are a beautiful rose-pink. This one was photographed between Langtry and Dryden in April. *Central and West Texas; abundant from Sonora to the Guadalupe Mountains. April–October, depending on location.*

———————————————

C. integra also grows in Central and West Texas. It is usually 6–16 inches tall. The leaves are narrow, unlobed, and undivided. The bracts are usually scarlet or cerise, sometimes yellow, mostly rounded on the outer edge. *Central and West Texas. April–October.*

Leucophyllum frutescens
Cenizo (Silverleaf, Barometer Bush)

Cenizo grows 3–6 feet high and is the commonest of 3 species of *Leucophyllum* found wild in Texas. The leaves are light gray-green, giving rise to the name "cenizo," meaning "ashy." The leaves are opposite, whorled, or alternate. The rose to orchid-rose flower has 5 sepals and 5 petals, which form a funnel-shaped flower about 1 inch across at the opening. The plant is sensitive to moisture and will bloom shortly after a rain, hence "barometer bush." It is often used as an ornamental. Photographed between Uvalde and Brackettville in July. *From Central Texas southwest to the Big Bend area and south to Mexico. June–October. Perennial.*

Another species, *L. candidum*, has flowers that are lavender to dark purple. It is found in scattered locations over the Trans-Pecos.

Penstemon cobaea
Large-flowered Beard Tongue (False Foxglove, Wild Foxglove)

Linaria texana
Toadflax

Toadflax is 1–3 feet tall and grows from a cluster of leaves at the base which are finely divided into somewhat rounded segments. Upper leaves are narrow to needle-like, alternate, and about 1 inch long. The blue flowers are loosely arranged on the upper third of the stem, having 5 petals that are united at the base and form a 2-lipped blossom about ½ inch long. The lower lip arches upward, almost closing the throat of the flower. It has a slender spur ½ inch long. This photograph was taken near Crockett in April. *Grows along roadsides, in uncultivated fields, and in open areas in East and Central Texas. March–May. Annual or winter biennial.*

Nearly all members of the Figwort Family have 4 stamens, but those in the genus *Penstemon* have 5. The fifth one does not have an anther and is often bearded; thus the name "beard tongue." *Penstemon* species grow all over Texas, and any part of the state can lay claim to at least one of them.

The large-flowered beard tongue grows 12–18 inches tall on a downy stem. Leaves are opposite and attach directly to the stem. Flowers are 1½–2 inches long and may be whitish, violet, or pink, usually with purple lines in the throat. They grow on the upper part of the stem, in loose clusters in the axils of the small upper leaves or bracts. We photographed this one near Sherman in May. *East and Central Texas. April–May. Perennial.*

Penstemon murrayanus
Scarlet Penstemon (Beard Tongue)

Scarlet penstemon grows to about 3 feet
high, with reddish stems and opposite
leaves. The upper ones are cup-shaped,
round, and attached directly to the stem,
encircling it completely. Leaves are
smooth on the edges and have a downy
covering. The flowering upper portion of
the stem is often over a foot long, with a
profusion of tubular, scarlet flowers about
1 inch long, opening into 5 petal-like
lobes. Stamens extend beyond the flower,
and the fifth stamen, which has no anther,
is lightly bearded. This specimen was photographed near Woodville in May. *Pine
woods and open prairies over most of East
Texas. March–June. Perennial.*

——————————————————

P. barbatus, beardlip penstemon, is similar to scarlet penstemon, with narrow,
pointed leaves and tubular flowers 1 inch
long, which often appear to be on only
1 side of the stem. The lower lip of the
flower is bent backward, and the upper lip
projects forward, making it strongly 2-
lipped. *Mountains of West Texas. June–
October. Perennial.*

Verbascum blattaria
Moth Mullein

Two species of mullein grow in Texas. They differ from some other members of the Figwort Family in that the flowers are radially, rather than bilaterally, symmetrical. Moth mullein is the smaller, more slender of the 2 species. Its stem and leaves are smooth. The leaves are toothed to lightly scalloped and attached directly to the stem. It grows 2–4 feet tall and often has 2–4 flowering branches below the flowering spike. The plant has 50–100 potential blossoms. The buds are pink, but the flowers are yellow, with 5 rounded petals (the lower ones are a little longer than the others), crimped on the edges and joined at the base. This joining makes for

an interesting feature in that the mature flower falls to the ground intact, including the 5 stamens. The stamens have yellow anthers, but the filament is covered with tiny orchid-colored hairs, giving the flower an orchid center. The name "moth mullein" comes from the resemblance of the hairy stamens and the pistil to the tongue and antennae of a moth. This plant is said to be common throughout the United States, but the only place we have ever seen it is on Loop 256 around Palestine, where we photographed it in late May. *Winter annual or biennial.*

Verbascum thapsus
Great Mullein (Common Mullein)

The great mullein produces in the first year a rosette of successively larger leaves toward the ground, and a deep tap root. The following spring a stiffly erect flower stem arises from the crown, terminating in a wandlike raceme of crowded yellow, or rarely white, flowers. The plant grows 2–7 feet tall, is usually unbranched, and has feltlike, pubescent leaves and stems. Leaves are 4–15 inches long, simple, alternate, and without stems. Flowers are in a raceme 6–36 inches long. They have 3 yellow petal-like lobes about ½ inch long and 5 sepals, united at the base. There are 5 stamens of unequal length, with reddish anthers. Photographed near Whitehouse in July. *Grows in sandy soils and neglected fields, chiefly in the eastern third of the state. June–September. Biennial.*

SOLANACEAE
Potato or Nightshade Family

Most of the plants in the Potato Family
are herbs with alternate leaves, which may
be toothed, pinnately lobed, or divided.
The identifying feature of the flowers is
the star-shaped or wheel-shaped corolla,
the 5 sepals and 5 petals being united. In
most genera the 5 long, bright-yellow
anthers form a narrow cone which protrudes conspicuously from the center of
the flower. The flowers may be white,
yellow, blue, or purple. The fruit is usually
a showy berry.

Cultivated plants of this family include
tomatoes, potatoes, sweet peppers, egg-
plant, belladonna, tobacco, and petunias.

Datura wrightii
Jimsonweed (Thorn Apple)

The large, white, trumpet-shaped jimson-
weed flower can be found from one end of
the state to the other and is always a re-
freshing surprise. Though it grows in varied habitats, one sees it only rarely. It is
a spreading, bushy plant, often 3 feet tall
and 5–8 feet across. The branches are
mainly on the upper half. The broad
leaves are 4–10 inches long on short
stems, with fine hair, especially along the
veins. The flowers sometimes have a pale
pinkish cast. The petals are united to
form a funnel 6–9 inches long and 2½–4
inches across, opening in the evening and
closing by mid-morning. On still eve-
nings, hawk moths are apt to be darting
from flower to flower. The whole plant is
poisonous, but, because of its bad odor and
taste, livestock seldom eat it. This one
was photographed 5 miles west of Canton
in April. *Statewide. May–November.
Perennial.*

Nicotiana glauca
Tobacco Tree

The tobacco "tree" grows up to 20 feet tall along the Rio Grande from Del Rio to El Paso. The branches grow alternately off the main stem, with flower clusters at the end of each one. Leaves are 3–4 inches long—longer on the main stem—all with leaf-stems about 1 inch long. They are broad at the base, sloping to a slender point. The leaves contain the alkaloid anabasine, which is poisonous to livestock. The greenish-yellow tubular flowers, 2–3 inches long, grow in clusters at the ends of the stems. Photographed at Hot Springs on the Rio Grande, in Big Bend National Park, in April. *South and West Texas. April–October. Perennial.*

Another species, *N. trigonophylla*, grows throughout the desert areas of the Southwest and was the tobacco used by the Indians. It is a much smaller plant than *N. glauca*.

Quincula lobata
Purple Ground-Cherry

Purple ground-cherry grows almost flat on
the ground. Leaves are alternate, 1½–3
inches long and not quite as broad, often
coarsely toothed or deeply cut, with
rounded lobes. The flower is bluish-
purple, with 5 united petals that open out
to form a flat surface ¾–1¼ inches across.
It has 5 stamens with yellow anthers. This
flower seems not to be much affected
by drought. It would be good as a garden
flower, especially in areas of little rainfall.
This one was photographed near Mason in
April. *Grows from Central Texas west
through the Trans-Pecos and Panhandle.
March–October. Perennial.*

————————————————

Yellow ground-cherry, *Physalis pumila,*
grows 1–2½ feet tall and is densely hairy.
Leaves are simple, oval, 1½–3 inches long
on leaf stems ¾–1½ inches long. There is
only 1 flower to a short stem which grows
from a leaf axil. When the flower first appears, the stem is erect, but later it begins
to bend slightly and the flower hangs its
head. The flower is ½ inch across or less,
yellow, slightly purplish at the base. *Eastern third of state. April–October.*

Solanum elaeagnifolium
**White Horse Nettle (Silverleaf Night-
shade, Trompillo)**

There are several species of horse nettle,
all of which have star-shaped blossoms
with prominent petals, flat or turned backward, and yellow stamens. Almost all of
them are prickly. Flowers of the various species are blue, purple, yellow, or
white.

White horse nettle gets its name from
its covering of silvery hairs, among which
are the nettle-like prickles. It grows 1–3
feet tall. The leaves are 2–4 inches long,
with wavy edges. Flowers are violet-purple
or white, about ¾ inch across, with 5
petal-like lobes that are joined at the base,
forming a triangular shape at the tip of
each lobe. All of them have the prominent, bright yellow stamens that distinguish all the horse nettles. The yellow
fruits resemble small tomatoes and remain on the plant for months. They are
said to be poisonous. Photographed near
Tyler in May. *Grows over most of Texas
and will thrive in very dry areas. March–
October. Perennial.*

STYRACACEAE
Storax or Snowball Family

The shrubs or small trees of the Storax Family have alternate leaves on short stems, simple, pinnately veined, entire, sharply toothed or slightly lobed. The calyx is cup-shaped and 4- or 5-toothed. The corolla has 4 or 5 white lobes, separate nearly to the base. There are 10 stamens and 1 pistil.

Halesia diptera
Silver Bell

The snow-white flowers of this slow-growing deciduous shrub are about 1 inch across and consist of 4 waxy petals with a tight cluster of stamens in the center, looking somewhat like a white candle in a white candle holder. Flowers grow in small clusters along the stem, each flower on a separate, short stem. The plant grows 3–15 feet high and has alternate leaves 2–7 inches long and half as wide, with distinct veins. The photograph was taken near Burkeville in April. *Southeast Texas. March–May. Perennial.*

THEACEAE
Camellia Family

The Camellia Family is characterized by trees or shrubs with alternate, simple, feather-veined leaves and no stipules. The flowers are regular. Both sepals and petals overlap in bud. The stamens are more or less united at the base with each other and with the base of the petals. There are few seeds. It is a family with showy flowers, the most familiar of which are the well-known camellia and the important tea plant. There are 5 white petals, ovate sepals, stamens with dark purple filaments and blue anthers, 1 style, and 5 toothed stigmas. The plants grow in rich woods.

Stewartia malacodendron
Silky Camellia

Silky camellia is a large, open-branched shrub growing up to 10 feet tall. Leaves are alternate, deciduous, 2–4 inches long and half as wide, silky below, and distinctly veined. Flowers are white to cream-colored, 2–3 inches across, and saucer-shaped. The petals are crimped at the margins and wider at the tip. The numerous black stamens are conspicuous. This plant is rare in Texas. This one was photographed in Newton County, East Texas, in May. Osa Hall, who worked for years with the Texas Forest Service, showed us the area where a number of them grew. It was his custom, except with persons he knew well, to blindfold people he took to this location lest they return to get specimens for transplanting. *East Texas. April–June. Perennial.*

UMBELLIFERAE (APIACEAE)
Parsley or Carrot Family

The Parsley Family can usually be recognized by the arrangement of the tiny flowers in umbels which are again clustered to form a compound umbel whose radiating stems suggest the ribs of an umbrella; hence, the Latin name Umbelliferae. Each of the tiny flowers that make up the umbrella-like clusters has 5 white or yellow petals, 5 stamens, and 1 pistil. Sometimes the sepals show 5 minute teeth. Leaves are alternately arranged and are usually divided into fine leaflets which are often much toothed. The stem is usually hollow. Cultivated members of this family include carrots, parsnips, dill, caraway, parsley, celery, and myrrh.

Conium maculatum
Poison Hemlock

The Parsley Family includes many edible plants, but this species is extremely poisonous. The Greeks put Socrates to death by requiring him to "drink the hemlock." It was widely used in the execution of criminals in ancient times, and one can easily be poisoned simply through careless handling of the plant. All parts of it are poisonous. Children have been poisoned by making whistles from the main stem, as they do with the elderberry.

The plant sometimes grows up to 10 feet tall. Leaves are pinnately divided and lobed, 12–18 inches long, distinctly toothed. The large flower heads are 6–8 inches across, consisting of several umbels growing from the same point, each umbel about 2 inches across with many small flowers ¹⁄₁₆ inch across with white petals. The stem is purple-spotted. We photographed this one near Tyler in May. *Grows in roadside ditches and uncultivated fields throughout East Texas; extends to the Trans-Pecos, where it is also abundant. Biennial.*

Daucus carota
Queen Anne's Lace (Wild Carrot)

Queen Anne's lace is very common along roadsides and in disturbed ground and can be found in almost any part of Texas. It is a beautiful flower, with a 2–6-inch flower head at the top of the stem, which is usually 2–3 feet tall. The large, umbrella-like head is made up of small umbels of tiny white blossoms ⅛ inch or less across. An odd characteristic is that the center blossom of the entire head is a deep wine-red. The plant has alternate leaves up to 6 inches long and about half as wide, divided into narrow segments, like the leaf of a carrot. (The cultivated carrot is a variety of this wild species.) When the flowers pass the blooming stage, the threadlike stems of the blossoms turn upward, giving the entire head the familiar "bird's nest" shape; when the seeds mature, the heads open again, spreading the seeds. This plant was photographed near Gilmer in May. *Abundant throughout Texas. May–July. Biennial.*

Eryngium heterophyllum
Mexican Thistle

This whole plant has a silvery thistle-look. The leaves, as well as the bracts around the flower, are bristle-toothed. It grows 1½–2 feet tall, with a heavy, stout stem densely branched on the upper half. The stems are smooth, but the leaves are divided into sharp lobes on each side of a midrib. The flowers are clustered on a more or less egg-shaped head, up to ⅗ inch long and smaller at the end and about ½ inch across. They are surrounded by showy, spiny leafbracts. When the tiny, silvery-looking flowers mature, they turn sky-blue. It is an attractive plant, suited for use in flower arrangements, as the flowers hold their form and color for an extended period, and can be handled easily enough if one is careful in cutting them. This photograph was taken in the Davis Mountains in September. *Trans-Pecos. August–October. Perennial.*

Eryngium leavenworthii
Eryngo (False Purple Thistle)

The eryngos are not true thistles, but anyone familiar with this spiny plant will
easily understand how it got the name.
The plant grows 1–3 feet high, often in
dense masses in fields or along roadsides,
as thistles do. In August the foliage is
gray-green, but it gradually takes on a purple hue by September. The flowers are
often used in dried arrangements. The
flower heads, up to 2 inches long, the
bracts, and the stamens are all purple. The
flowers grow on short stems in the forks
of the branches. The deeply lobed leaves
surround the stem, clasping it, and the
leaf segments have many spiny teeth. A
tuft of small, rigid, spiny leaves grows out
of the top of the flower head. It is desirable
to wear a thick pair of gloves if one cuts
the flowers. We photographed this one between Austin and Temple in September.
Abundant in Central Texas. August–
September. Perennial.

Hydrocotyle bonariensis
Salt Pennywort

Salt pennywort is a fleshy plant, 6–10
inches tall, with round, undivided leaves,
2–4 inches across, attached to the stem in
the center of the leaf. The leaf edge is scalloped. The flower head is an umbel 2–3
inches across. Individual flowers are tiny,
with 5 greenish-to-white petals. Photographed on the coast between Galveston
and High Island in April. *Abundant along*
the Gulf in sandy soils extending from
high-tide level inland; adapted to salty,
brackish marshes. March–May. Perennial.

Polytaenia nuttalli
Wild Dill (Prairie Parsley, Prairie Parsnip)

Wild dill has stiff, stout stems, usually 2 feet high, which become dry and brown and remain standing through the winter months. The leaves are 1–3 inches long and nearly as broad, deeply cut, and lobed. Upper leaves usually have 3 lobes, lower ones 5. The flowers are small, ¼ inch across, greenish-yellow, and grow in umbel-like clusters, 2 inches across, branching irregularly from the leaf axils near the top of the plant. Photographed between Rockport and the Aransas National Wildlife Refuge in April. *On prairies throughout the state. April–May. Biennial.*

Zizia aurea
Golden Alexanders

We have found golden Alexanders scattered over East Texas, but more commonly on the northeastern prairies from Bonham eastward. The showy plant, up to 4 feet tall, has many branches. The compound leaves are divided into leaflets, which are also divided, deeply cut, and fine-toothed. The upper leaves are smaller, with 1–3 flower stems growing from the axils. The flower heads are a compound umbel of yellow flowers less than ⅛ inch long. Each tiny flower has 5 sepals, 5 petals, and 5 stamens. Photographed near Paris in May. *East and Northeast Texas. May–July. Perennial.*

VERBENACEAE
Vervain Family

At least 7 genera of the Vervain Family are found in Texas. *Verbena* is by far the largest, with at least 10 species. The flowers in most members of the family have 5 petals, joined with slightly unequal lobes; 4 stamens in 2 pairs of unequal length; and a 4-lobed ovary. One exception is the genus *Phyla*, with 4 petals and a 2-lobed ovary. (In order to make a positive identification in some of the species of Mints, Figworts, and Vervains, one would have to dissect the ovary.) Leaves are paired or whorled and undivided, though they may be toothed.

Aloysia gratissima
Whitebrush (Beebrush)

Whitebrush is a thicket-forming western shrub 3–14 feet tall, much-branched, slender, and aromatic. The wood is yellow. When it is in bloom, about all one sees is a profusion of white flowers that almost conceal the stems. Flower stems grow at frequent intervals from the many branches, with flower clusters 1–3 inches long. The shrubs grow most commonly along the arroyos and overflow areas west of the Pecos River, and bloom shortly after a rain, the flowers lasting several days. They are very fragrant. An excellent, light-colored honey made from the flowers took first prize at the Chicago World Fair. The Big Bend country is noted for it, and we have bought whitebrush honey for 25 years from Mr. W. E. Gillespie at Presidio. Photographed in the Chisos Mountains in September. *South, Central, and West Texas. March–November. Perennial.*

Callicarpa americana
French Mulberry (American Beauty Berry)

It is not so much the flowers as the berries of the French mulberry that attract people's attention. The shrub grows 3–5 feet tall, with several branches. Leaves are opposite, 3–6 inches long, the upper surface wrinkled with sunken veins and the edges fine-toothed. When the leaves are bruised, even slightly, they give off a delightful, woodsy, pungent odor.

The flower cluster and, later, the berries are in the axil of the leaves, surrounding the stem in a firm, tight cluster. Flowers are ⅛–¼ inch across, pale pink, with stamens extended much beyond the petals. The berries are ¼ inch across and hold their shape and color for weeks; for that reason they are excellent in flower arrangements. The plant itself is most suitable in landscaping large gardens.

Many birds feed on the berries and will contend with each other to include a bush in their feeding area. Leaves wilt quickly and fall off, leaving an attractive, somewhat formally arranged stalk of berries up

to 2½ feet long. The fruit turns reddish-purple in September or October, occasionally while the plant is still flowering, and remains until frost, or later, if the birds have not eaten it. Photographed in our yard near Whitehouse. *Grows in woods all over East Texas. May–September. Perennial.*

Lantana horrida
Texas Lantana

Texas lantana is a common native species with bright, attractive orange-and-yellow flowers that turn red with age. Plants grow 3–5 feet tall with slightly prickly stems and opposite leaves, 1½–4 inches long. It blooms in dense heads at the ends of stems growing out of the leaf axils. Each tiny flower, ¼–⅓ inch long, has 4 or 5 petals that unite to form a funnel shape ¼ inch across at the opening. This attractive flower grows under widely differing conditions and lends color to anyone's garden. We photographed this one near Gilmer in May. *Blooms most of the year in South Texas, April–October throughout East and Central Texas, and a little earlier in the Trans-Pecos. Perennial.*

— — — — — — — — — — — — — —

L. camara is mainly a cultivated plant, but some have escaped. Flowers are cream-colored and pink with a yellow center. *Eastern half of state, sometimes to the Trans-Pecos. May–July. Perennial.*

Verbena bipinnatifida
Prairie Verbena

There are many species of *Verbena* in Texas, and they are difficult to identify. Once one becomes familiar with the blossom, however, it will be easy to recognize the genus *Verbena* wherever it is seen. We have photographed species in Alaska, in the driest part of the Nevada desert, and in lush East Texas; and the only difference a lay observer would notice is a slightly different shade of purple in the flowers.

Prairie verbena is one of the most abundant and familiar wildflowers of Texas, growing throughout most of the state. It is also one of the first to attract attention in early spring, when it blooms along roads, in fields, and in open woods under widely varying conditions. It is an erect to sprawling plant, 6–16 inches tall, with many branches. The lower branches sprawl or creep along the ground and take root wherever a joint touches, forming dense colonies. Recently we photographed a 10-acre plot in full bloom just off Route 281 in Central Texas. Leaves are opposite and deeply cut several times on both sides of

the midrib; they are 1–3½ inches long and 1½ inches wide on a 1-inch stem. The bluish-purple flower clusters grow at the ends of the stems. Individual flowers are about ½ inch long and ½ inch wide at the opening, with 5 sepals and 5 petals. Photographed at Lake Tyler in April. *East Texas. March–July. Perennial.*

—————————————

The flowers of tuber vervain, *V. rigida,* grow in short, dense, cylindrical clusters at the end of the stems. They are purple to reddish-purple and trumpet-shaped, ending in 5 petal-like lobes. The clusters are 1–2 inches long. The plant grows 1–2 feet tall, usually with 2–4 short branches near the top, and often forms colonies. Leaves are opposite, 1½–4½ inches long and 1 inch or more wide. They are coarsely but sharply toothed. *East and Central Texas and along the coastal plains. April–October. Perennial.*

Verbena halei
Texas Vervain (Slender Vervain)

The tall, erect *Verbena* species, commonly called vervain, are hard to identify, but if one observes their tiny flowers and the way they grow on the stem, it will at least be clear that they belong to one of the erect *Verbena* species.

Texas vervain is widely distributed, and we have photographed it all over the state in April and May. It is an erect plant 1–2½ feet tall, with several branches in the upper part. The leaves vary widely, with the bottom leaves deeply cut in some cases and the upper leaves slightly toothed, or sometimes with smooth margins. Leaves are ¾–3 inches long and 1½ inches wide. There are several small flowers in long, loose clusters, blooming around the stem from the bottom up, usually 6–20 flowers blooming at the same time. They are bluish to lavender, ¼ inch across, trumpet-shaped, ending in 5 petal-like lobes. Photographed east of Austin in April. *Statewide, in meadows and fields or along roadsides. February–November. Perennial.*

VIOLACEAE
Violet Family

Members of the Violet Family are not hard to identify as a group, for they are all small plants with a distinct "butterfly," or bilateral, corolla. The 2 side petals are narrow; 2 upper petals are usually erect; those 4 usually have stripes of a bright color to guide insects to the nectar inside; and the fifth petal, the lowest, has a hollow spur extending backward. There are 5 sepals. Filaments of the stamens are short, and the anthers are close together, or united. Leaves of some violets are alternate on the stems; some are crowded close to the base of the stem. Some violets have "beards," or hairs, on the side and bottom petals that keep out rain and give insects a place to land. Violets hybridize frequently, forming vigorous new forms. They are easy to transplant.

Viola missouriensis
Missouri Violet

Walking through the woods in early spring, one is not surprised to see the Missouri violet pushing its way up through dead leaves or other vegetation, rarely more than 2 or 3 plants in one place. They have 5 petals, like all violets, deep to pale violet in color. The 2 lateral petals are bearded. The heart-shaped leaves, coarsely toothed, have long stems growing from the base. This was photographed south of Tyler in March. *Eastern third of state. March–April. Perennial.*

————————————————

Another species, *V. bicolor*, wild pansy, also grows in East and Northeast Texas, blooming in early March. We always seem to have a special appreciation for it because it is one of the very early flowers to announce the advent of spring. It is deep violet to pale lavender in color. Its leaves grow in clusters on the stem, and out of them grow 1 or 2 leafless stems with a blossom at the end. This is one of the smallest of Texas violets. *Grows in sandy soil all over East Texas. Mostly in March. Annual.*

V. papilionacea has heart-shaped leaves with blunt-toothed edges and smooth stems, each bearing 1 blossom. The long-stemmed, simple leaf grows from the base of the plant. Flowers have 5 petals, varying from light to deep violet. The 2 side petals have beards, or tufts of white hairs. *Grows mostly in shaded places in the eastern half of the state. Early spring. Perennial.*

Viola pedata
Bird's-Foot Violet

The greatest concentration of bird's-foot violets we have seen was on the banks of Village Creek, in the Big Thicket area, where it almost covered the bank for 300 feet. It is one of the largest Texas violets, 4–6 inches tall. The leaves, almost round in outline, are ¾–2 inches long, deeply cut into 3–5 segments, and these again narrowly lobed. The leaf stem is 4–6 inches long. Flowers are pale to dark purple, broad, flat, 1–1½ inches across. They have 5 petals, the 2 upper ones smaller than the lower 3 and deep violet. The lowest petal has the dark streakings which are common to most violets. There are 5 stamens with brilliant orange anthers. Photographed south of Burkeville in March. *Southeast Texas. March–April. Perennial.*

Another species, *V. triloba*, has leaves broader than they are long, with 3–7 lobes, the middle lobe much broader than the others. Flowers are up to 1½ inches across. The 5 violet-purple petals have darker streakings. *East and North-Central Texas. March–April. Perennial.*

ZYGOPHYLLACEAE
Caltrop Family

The herbs and shrubs of the Caltrop Family have 4 or 5 petals, which may be blue, white, orange, or yellow in Texas species. The leaves are borne singly or in pairs and are variously divided. Flowers are in the axils of the leaves. There are usually twice as many stamens as petals, and the pistil has the same number of parts as there are petals, or twice as many.

Kallstroemia grandiflora
Orange Caltrop (Desert Poppy)

Orange caltrop grows 2–3 feet tall, sometimes more, and its several branches are quite hairy. It is inclined to spread and is often seen in clumps 2–5 feet across. Leaves are opposite and compound, with 5–10 pairs of leaflets about 1 inch long on each side of the midrib, like the feather of a bird. It is a favorite bird food, especially liked by doves. The yellow-orange flowers, often 2½ inches in diameter, have 5 petals, 5 sepals, and 10 stamens. It is easy to confuse this flower with some of the mallows, but the stamens of the mallow often join, forming a column and making the center of the flower very prominent, while the stamens of orange caltrop remain separate. Photographed west of Terlingua in September. *Southwest Texas. March–October.*

Larrea tridentata
Creosote Bush (Greasewood)

The creosote bush is one of the commonest plants of the desert, and almost anyone can readily identify it by its odor. A crushed leaf smells like creosote; hence its common name. The plant grows 4–6 feet tall, has many branches, and is evergreen. The small, compound leaves, ⅕–⅖ inch long, are composed of 2 leaflets. They are opposite, united at the base, pointed at the tip, dark to yellowish-green, strongscented, and often sticky with resin. The plant is an indicator of poor soil and has the ability to survive under extremely unfavorable conditions. This and the fact that it is not eaten by animals enable it to extend its range at the expense of other plants. In addition, creosote plants produce a chemical in roots and leaves which inhibits germination of seeds, thus reducing competition. The flowers are yellow and inconspicuous except under favorable conditions, when they are prominent, giv-

ing the bush a yellowish cast. They are ¼–½ inch long, with 5 petals, 10 stamens, and 1 pistil. This photograph was taken in Big Bend National Park in April. *West Texas. Usually blooms April–May, often much later after good rains. Perennial.*

Porlieria angustifolia
Guayacán

A leafy, compact evergreen, guayacán rarely grows higher than 6 feet, though under favorable conditions it may grow twice that high. It is often darker than surrounding shrubs, due to the stems being covered with dark green leaves. Leaves are pinnately compound, with 4–8 pairs of small, leathery leaflets. Flowers, which have 5 petals, are violet to purple, 1 inch across, with prominent yellow anthers. The blossom is followed by small, heart-shaped pods that burst open at maturity, exposing 2 scarlet-red, shiny seeds. The bark of the roots is sometimes used as soap for washing woolen goods, as it does not fade colors. Guayacán is also a good honeybee plant. It does best at elevations below 4,000 feet, though we have photographed healthy specimens in the Chisos

Basin on the slopes of Pulliam Mountain. This one was photographed in Green Gulch in the Chisos Mountains in April. *West and Southwest Texas. April–October. Perennial.*

Glossary

NOTE: *See illustrated glossary for figure references.*

Alternate Placed singly at different heights on the stem; not opposite or whorled. (Fig. 7*a*)

Annual Growing from seed to maturity and dying in one year or season.

Anther The pollen-bearing part of the flower. (Fig. 1)

Areole A spot in the form of a pit or a raised area on the surface of a cactus through which spines or other structures grow. (Fig. 13)

Axil The upper angle between any two structures or organs, as where a leaf or branch joins the stem. (Fig. 6*a*)

Basal leaves The leaves that are concentrated near the base of the main stem.

Beard A tuft or line of hairs, as on certain petals. (Fig. 4*d*)

Biennial A plant that takes two years to complete the flowering cycle. Typically it grows leaves the first year and flowers and leaves the second.

Bilateral symmetry The flower must be divided in half lengthwise for the two sides to be identical. (Fig. 2*b*)

Blade The expanded portion of a leaf or petal. (Fig. 6*a*)

Bract A reduced or modified leaf occurring at the base of a flower or group of flowers. Bracts are sometimes arranged in rows, like shingles on a roof, usually closely cupping the blossoms of Compositae (Sunflower Family); see also *Phyllaries*. Sometimes brightly colored or petallike, as in *Castilleja* (paintbrush), or threadlike, as in *Daucus carota* (Queen Anne's lace). (Fig. 5*d*)

Bristly Having stiff, rigid, rather thick hairs on the surface of stems or leaves.

Calyx The sepals taken collectively. These may be distinct, or joined to form a cup or tube; they may be of any color but are usually green. When the calyx is present, it encloses the other parts of the flower in bud. (Fig. 1)

Complete flower A flower with sepals, petals, stamens, and pistil present. (Fig. 1)

Compound leaf A leaf that is completely separated into two or more leaflets. (Fig. 10)

Corm A short, fleshy underground stem, broader than high, producing stems from the base and leaves and flower stems from the top.

Corolla The petals collectively; usually colored or showy. These may be distinct or united to form a cup, trumpet, tube, or two-lipped body. (Fig. 1)

Corymb A flat-topped or convex flower cluster, with the lower or outer stems longer; the flowers on these stems open first. (Fig. 5*f*)

Cyme A usually flattish inflorescence in which the central or terminal flower matures first. (Fig. 5*i*)

Deciduous Having leaves that all fall off at the end of the growing season, or at least wither up and become lifeless.

Disc flowers The inner tubular flowers on the heads of Compositae (Sunflower Family). (Fig. 3)

Entire Said of margins without teeth or lobes. (Fig. 9*a*)

Escape A cultivated plant that has gone wild.

Evergreen Remaining green and leafy through the winter.

Filament Stalk of stamen; bears the anther. (Fig. 1)

Floret A small flower, especially one in a dense cluster.

Flower head A dense arrangement of flowers arising from a common point, as in the Umbelliferae, or as in the Compositae where many ray flowers and/or disc flowers make up one "flower head." (Figs. 3*a*, 5*f*, *g*)

Imperfect flower A flower lacking either stamens or pistil.

Incomplete flower A flower lacking one or more of the following: stamens, pistil, petals, sepals.

Inferior ovary An ovary situated below the origin of sepals and petals. In many species the ovary is below the point of attachment of all the other parts of the flower, i.e., embedded in the flower stem. It usually shows as a swelling below the flower and may be seen only by cutting through this swelling.

Inflorescence A complete flower cluster or flower head, including bracts.

Internode The part of the stem between leaves or branches.

Involucre A whorl of distinct or united leaves or bracts beneath a flower or cluster of flowers. (Fig. 5g, h)

Irregular flower A flower unequal in the size, form, or union of its similar parts; bilaterally symmetrical. Example: Leguminosae (Legume Family). (Fig. 2b)

Lobe Part or segment of a flower or leaf; a deep indentation that does not break the continuity of the structure.

Lobed flower A tubular or funnel-shaped flower that opens into petal-like lobes. (Fig. 4)

Lobed leaf A leaf with indentations not more than halfway to the midrib, with the tips of the segments rounded. (Fig. 9c, d)

Midrib The main or central rib or vein of a leaf.

Node The place on a stem where leaves or branches normally originate; a swollen or knoblike structure. (Fig. 6a)

Opposite Said of leaves originating in pairs at a node, with the members of each pair opposite each other on the stem. (Fig. 7b)

Ovary The basal part of the pistil, bearing the ovules, which later develop into seeds. (Fig. 1) See also *Inferior ovary; Superior ovary.*

Palmate Divided or radiating from one point, resembling a hand with the fingers spread. Leaves may be *palmately compound* and/or *palmately lobed;* they may also have *palmate venation.* (Figs. 8d, 9d, 10b)

Panicle A branched raceme; a raceme of racemes. (Fig. 5e)

Pappus In Compositae (Sunflower Family), a modified calyx, commonly appearing as hairs, bristles, or bumps, and usually persisting on the fruit. (Fig. 3)

Parallel venation Main veins running from base to apex of leaf. (Fig. 8b)

Pedicel The stalk of a single flower in a cluster of flowers. (Fig. 5d–g)

Peduncle The stalk of a solitary flower or of a cluster of flowers. (Fig. 5d–i)

Perennial Living for more than two years.

Perfect flower A flower with both stamens and pistil; it may or may not have corolla and/or calyx.

Perianth Collective term for petals and sepals (corolla and calyx).

Petal Unit of the corolla.

Petiole A leaf stem. (Figs. 6a, 7a, 10a)

Phyllaries A term sometimes used for individual bracts below the head of flowers in Compositae (Sunflower Family), so designated to avoid confusion with bracts on the flower stem. (Fig. 3a)

Pinnate Arranged along an axis. Leaves may be *pinnately compound* (see below) and/or *pinnately lobed;* they may also have *pinnate venation,* with veins extending from the midrib. (Figs. 8c, 9c, 10a)

Pinnately compound leaves Leaves with leaflets opposite each other on each side of the midrib, like a bird's feather. They may be *oddly pinnate,* ending with a leaflet at the tip, or *evenly pinnate,* with no leaflet at the end. These leaflets may be twice compound, like the leaves on the sensitive briar (*Schrankia uncinata*). (Fig. 10a)

Pistil The seed-producing or female organ, consisting of ovary, style, and stigma; usually located in the center of the flower. (Fig. 1)

Pistillate flower A flower with pistil(s) but no stamens.

Pubescent Said of stems or leaves with soft hairs.

Raceme An inflorescence in which each flower is attached to the main stalk by a short stem (pedicel). The youngest flowers, at the tip, may continue to develop while those below are forming fruit. (Fig. 5d)

Radial symmetry The flower can be cut into two equal halves in many ways, provided that the plane of cutting passes through the center. (Fig. 2*a*)

Ray flowers The outer irregular flowers in the heads of many Compositae (Sunflower Family). Each has a single, tongue-shaped corolla. (Fig. 3)

Receptacle End of stem to which flowers are attached. (Fig. 1)

Regular flower A flower equal in size, form, and union of its similar parts; radially symmetrical. Example: Solanaceae (Potato Family).

Rib (of cactus) A ridge; a raised surface running vertically or sometimes spiraling, and bearing areoles in a row along its summit. Often thought of as being composed of more or less united tubercles which may be evident as bulging masses along it. (Fig. 13*c*)

Rosette An arrangement of leaves radiating from the stem at a nearly common level, frequently at or just above the ground line. (Fig. 7*b*)

Scape A naked flower stem rising from the ground. (Fig. 5*a*)

Scorpioid Curled, like the tail of a scorpion.

Sepals Parts that surround the petals, stamens, and pistil; usually green and leaf-like (Fig. 1). Sometimes they are the same size, shape, and color as the petals; as in *Cooperia pedunculata* (rain lily), in which case both sepals and petals are called *tepals.*

Sessile Lacking a stalk of any kind: a flower without a pedicel or a leaf without a petiole. (Figs. 5*c*, 6*b*, 7*b*, *c*)

Solitary Borne singly; alone. (Fig. 5*a*, *b*)

Spike Flowers are attached directly to the main stem; no pedicels are present. The youngest flowers or buds are at the top. (Fig. 5*c*)

spp Abbreviation for plural of "species."

Spur A tubular or saclike extension of a sepal or petal, usually containing nectar. (Fig. 5*j*)

Stamens The male parts of the flower, carrying the pollen; usually in the center of the blossom and surrounding the pistil, if present. Filaments and anthers collectively. (Fig. 1)

Staminate flower A flower with stamens but no pistil.

Stigma The tip of the pistil, which receives the pollen; may be rounded, lobed, or branched. (Fig. 1)

Stipule A basal appendage of the petiole; usually in pairs. Varies in shape and may be minute and hairlike or stiff and sharp, or like segments of the leaf blade. (Fig. 6*a*)

Style The stalk-like part of the pistil, connecting the ovary and the stigma. (Fig. 1)

Superior ovary An ovary situated above the origin of sepals and petals. (Fig. 1)

Tepals Collective term for sepals and petals when sepals are petal-like, as in *Cooperia pedunculata* (rain lily).

Toothed Said of petals or leaves having margins more or less sharply indented. (Fig. 9*b*)

Tubercle A more or less pyramidal knob rising from the stem surface of a cactus and having an areole on or near its summit. (Fig. 13*b*)

Two-lipped flower A flower that has an upper and a lower division, as in Labiatae (Mint Family). (Fig. 4*d*)

Umbel A rounded or flat-topped cluster of flowers on stems that radiate from the tip of the main stem. A *compound umbel* has smaller umbels at the ends of the radiating stems. (Fig. 5*g*, *h*)

Whorled leaves or flowers Three or more leaves or flowers arranged in a circle around a stem. (Fig. 7*c*)

Winter annual A plant from autumn-germinating seeds that fruits the following spring.

Illustrated Glossary

NOTE: *Terms are defined in the alphabetical glossary.*

Fig. 1.   Flower Parts

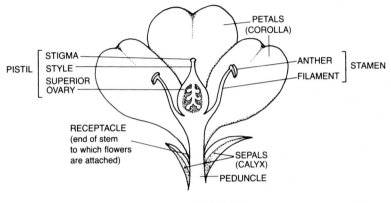

COMPLETE FLOWER

Fig. 2.   Flower Symmetry

a. Radial Symmetry   *b. Bilateral Symmetry*

Fig. 3. Section through a Composite Flower Head

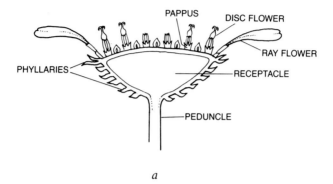

a

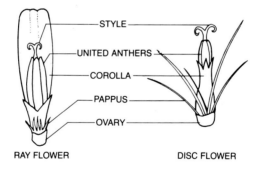

b   *c*

Fig. 4. Flower Shapes

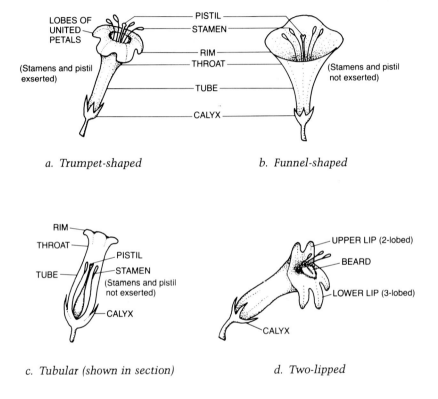

a. Trumpet-shaped   *b. Funnel-shaped*

c. Tubular (shown in section)   *d. Two-lipped*

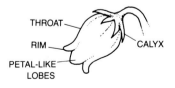

e. Urn-shaped   *f. Bell-shaped*

Fig. 5. Arrangement of Flowers on Stem

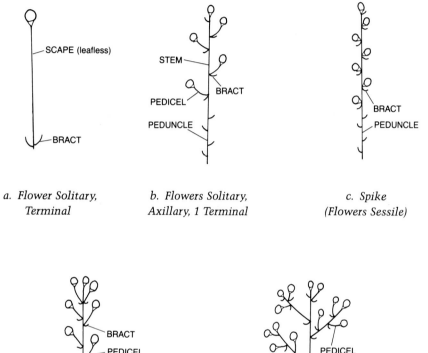

a. *Flower Solitary,*
Terminal

b. *Flowers Solitary,*
Axillary, 1 Terminal

c. *Spike*
(Flowers Sessile)

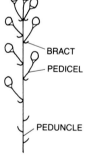

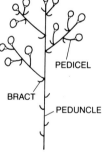

d. *Raceme*
(Flowers Pediceled)

e. *Panicle*
(Branched Raceme)

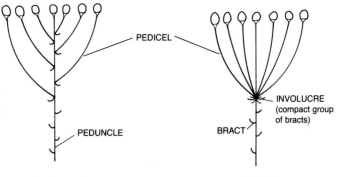

f. Corymb   g. Umbel

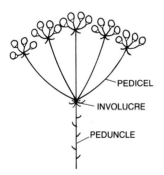 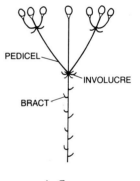

h. Compound Umbel   i. Cyme

SEPAL SPURRED   COROLLA SPURRED

j. Spur

Fig. 6.   Leaf Parts

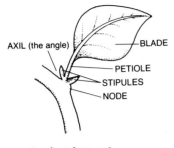

    a. Leaf with Petiole   b. Sessile Leaf (with no Petiole)

Fig. 7.   Leaf Arrangement

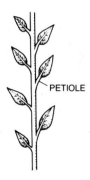
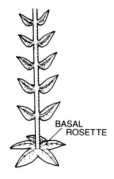

a. Alternate, Petioled   b. Opposite, Sessile   c. Whorled, Sessile
                                                            (3 or more at node)

Fig. 8. Venation (Vein Pattern)

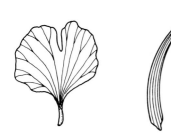

a. Forking

b. Parallel
(Main veins run
from base to apex)

c. Pinnate
(Main veins extend
from midrib)

d. Palmate
(Main veins radiate
from base)

Fig. 9. Simple Leaves

a. Entire

b. Toothed

c. Pinnately Lobed

d. Palmately Lobed

Fig. 10. Once Compound Leaves

a. Pinnately Compound

b. Palmately Compound

c. Trifoliate

Fig. 11. Leaf Types

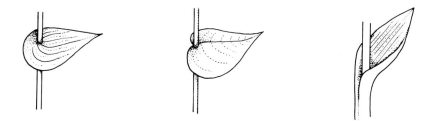

a. *Encircling*   b. *Clasping*   c. *Sheathing*

Fig. 12. Leaf Shapes

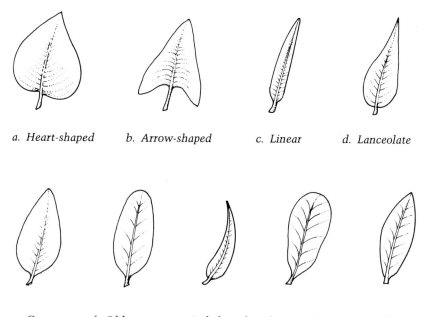

a. *Heart-shaped*   b. *Arrow-shaped*   c. *Linear*   d. *Lanceolate*

e. *Ovate*   f. *Oblong*   g. *Awl-shaped*   h. *Spatulate*   i. *Elliptic*

(A combination of two terms indicates a shape between them.)

Fig. 13. Cactus Parts

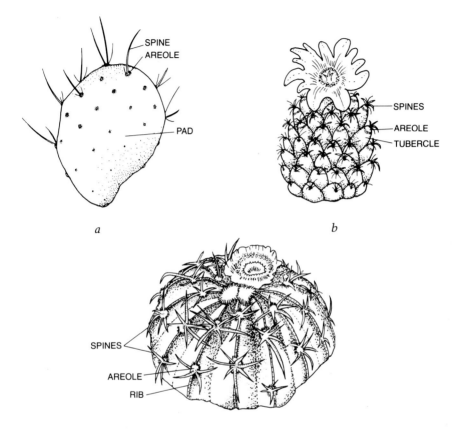

a   *b*

c

Bibliography Ajilvsgi, Geyata. 1979. *Wildflowers of the Big Thicket, East Texas, and Western Louisiana*. College Station and London: Texas A&M University Press.

Brown, Clair A. 1972. *Wildflowers of Louisiana and Adjoining States*. Baton Rouge: Louisiana State University Press.

Correll, D. S., and M. C. Johnston. 1970. *Manual of the Vascular Plants of Texas*. Renner: Texas Research Foundation.

Dodge, Natt N. 1963. *100 Desert Wildflowers in Natural Color*. Globe, Ariz.: Southwestern Monuments Association.

Gray, Asa. 1899. *Manual of Botany*. 6th ed. Edited by Watson Sereno. New York, Cincinnati, Chicago: American Book Co.

Harrington, H. D., and L. W. Durrell. 1957. *How to Identify Plants*. Chicago: Swallow Press.

Jaeger, Edmund C. 1940. *Desert Wild Flowers*. Stanford, Calif.: Stanford University Press.

McDougall, W. B., and Omer E. Sperry. 1957. *Plants of the Big Bend National Park*. Washington, D.C.: U.S. Government Printing Office.

Porter, C. L. 1967. *Taxonomy of Flowering Plants*. 2d ed. San Francisco: Freeman and Co.

Reeves, Robert G. 1972. *Flora of Central Texas*. Ft. Worth: Prestige Press.

Rickett, Harold William. 1969. *Wildflowers of the United States*, vol. 3, *Texas*. New York: McGraw-Hill.

Shinners, Lloyd A. 1972. *Spring Flora of the Dallas–Ft. Worth Area*. 2d ed. Edited by W. F. Mahler. Fort Worth: Prestige Press.

Stefferud, Alfred. 1950–1953. *How to Know the Wild Flowers*. New York: New American Library of World Literature.

Vines, Robert A. 1960. *Trees, Shrubs, and Woody Vines of the Southwest*. Austin: University of Texas Press.

Warnock, Barton H. 1970. *Wildflowers of the Big Bend Country, Texas*. Alpine, Tex.: Sul Ross State University.

———. 1974. *Wildflowers of the Guadalupe Mountains and the Sand Dune Country, Texas*. Alpine, Tex.: Sul Ross State University.

———. 1977. *Wildflowers of the Davis Mountains and Marathon Basin, Texas*. Alpine, Tex.: Sul Ross State University.

Weniger, Del. 1970. *Cacti of the Southwest: Texas, New Mexico, Oklahoma, Arkansas, and Louisiana*. Austin: University of Texas Press.

Wharton, Mary E., and Roger W. Barbour. 1971. *A Guide to the Wildflowers and Ferns of Kentucky*. Lexington: University Press of Kentucky.

Whitehouse, Eula. 1936. *Texas Flowers in Natural Colors*. Austin: Privately published.

———. 1962. *Common Fall Flowers of the Coastal Big Bend of Texas*. Sinton, Tex.: Bob and Bessie Welder Wildlife Foundation.

Wills, Mary Motz, and Howard S. Irwin. 1961. *Roadside Flowers of Texas*. Austin: University of Texas Press.

Index

258

INDEX

azalea
    hammock-sweet, 94
    honeysuckle, 94
    swamp, 94
    wild, 94

baby blue eyes, Texas, 107
baby peppers, 190
bachelor's button, 50; 195
baileya, desert, 48
Baileya multiradiata, 48
Baptisia
    leucophaea, 122
    sphaerocarpa, 122
Barberry Family, 16–17
barometer bush, 219
basket flower, 50
bean
    Cherokee, 128
    coral, 128
Bean Family, 118–140
beard flower, 180
beard tongue, 221
    large-flowered, 220
beebalm, 112
    lemon, 111
bee blossom, 174
beebrush, 233
beggar's ticks, 127
bell, silver, 227
bells, yellow, 20
Berberidaceae, 16–17
Berberis trifoliolata, 17
bergamot, wild, 112
Berlandiera lyrata, 49
Bignonia capreolata, 18
Bignoniaceae, 18–20
bird-of-paradise, 123
black-eyed Susan, 75
bladder-pod, Fendler, 88
bladderwort, floating, 141
Bladderwort Family, 141
blazing star, 64; 155
Bleeding-Heart Family, 100
bloodroot, 97
Bluebell Family, 36–37
bluebonnet
    Big Bend, 130
    Texas, 131

blue curls, 107
blue-eyed grass, 109
blue star, 10
bluet, 213
Boerhavia linearifolia, 169
bog violet, 141
boneset, blue, 56
Borage Family, 21–22
Boraginaceae, 21–22
bouvardia, scarlet, 212
Bouvardia ternifolia, 212
broomweed
    common, 81
    gummy, 82
    threadleaf, 81
brown-eyed Susan, 75
buckeye
    Mexican, 214
    red, 105
    Southern, 105
    Western, 105
    yellow, 105
Buckeye Family, 105; 214
buckwheat, wild, 197
Buckwheat Family, 196–197
bull nettle, Texas, 95
burhead, 2
bush pea, 122
buttercup, 207
    large-flowered, 207
    rough-seed, 207
Buttercup Family, 203–207
butter daisy, 79
butterfly weed, 16
butterweed, yellow-top, 76
butterwort, small, 141
Butterwort Family, 141
buttonbush, 213

Cactaceae, 22–35
cactus
    barrel, 29
    cane, 31
    catclaw, 29
    cholla, 31
    Christmas, 32
    claret cup, 26
    cone, 30
    devil's head, 23